MG TD
1949-1953

Compiled by
R.M. Clarke

ISBN 0 946 489 017

Distributed by
Brooklands Book Distribution Ltd.
'Holmerise', Seven Hills Road,
Cobham, Surrey, England

BROOKLANDS ROAD & TRACK SERIES

Road & Track on Corvette 1953-1967
Road & Track on Corvette 1968-1982
Road & Track on Ferrari 1968-1974
Road & Track on Ferrari 1975-1981
Road & Track on Fiat Sports Car 1968-1981
Road & Track on Jaguar 1974-1982
Road & Track on Lamborghini 1964-1982
Road & Track on Lotus 1972-1983
Road & Track on Mercedes Sports & GT Cars 1970-1980
Road & Track on Porsche 1972-1975
Road & Track on Porsche 1975-1978
Road & Track on Porsche 1979-1982

BROOKLANDS MUSCLE CARS SERIES

American Motors Muscle Cars 1966-1970
Camaro Muscle Cars 1966-1972
Chevrolet Muscle Cars 1966-1971
Dodge Muscle Cars 1967-1970
Mini Muscle Cars 1961-1979
Plymouth Muscle Cars 1966-1971
Muscle Cars Compared 1966-1971
Muscle Cars Compared Book 2 1965-1971

BROOKLANDS MILITARY VEHICLES SERIES

Allied Military Vehicles Collection No. 1
Jeep Collection No. 1

BROOKLANDS BOOKS SERIES

AC Cobra 1962-1969
Alfa Romeo Spider 1966-1981
Armstrong Siddeley Cars 1945-1960
Austin 7 in the Thirties
Austin Seven Cars 1930-1935
Austin 10 1932-1939
Austin A30 & A35 1951-1962
Austin Healey 100 1952-1959
Austin Healey 3000 1959-1967
Austin Healey 100 & 3000 Collection No. 1
Austin Healey Sprite 1958-1971
Avanti 1962-1983
BMW Six Cylinder Coupés 1969-1975
BMW 1600 Collection No. 1
BMW 2002 Collection No. 1
Buick Cars 1929-1939
Cadillac in the Sixties No. 1
Camaro 1966-1970
Chrysler Cars 1930-1939
Citroen Traction Avant 1934-1957
Citroen 2CV 1949-1982
Corvair 1959-1968
Corvette Cars 1955-1964
Daimler Dart & V-8 250 1959-1969
Datsun 240z & 260z 1970-1977
De Tomaso Collection No. 1
Dodge Cars 1924-1938
Ferrari Cars 1946-1956
Ferrari Cars 1957-1962
Ferrari Cars 1962-1966
Ferrari Cars 1966-1969
Ferrari Cars 1969-1973
Ferrari Cars 1973-1977
Ferrari Cars 1977-1981
Ferrari Collection No. 1
Fiat X1/9 1972-1980
Ford GT40 1964-1978
Ford Mustang 1964-1967
Ford Mustang 1967-1973
Ford RS Escort 1968-1980
Hudson & Railton Cars 1936-1940
Jaguar (& S.S) Cars 1931-1937
Jaguar (& S.S) Cars 1937-1947
Jaguar Cars 1948-1951
Jaguar Cars 1951-1953
Jaguar Cars 1955-1957
Jaguar Cars 1957-1961
Jaguar Cars 1961-1964
Jaguar Cars 1964-1968
Jaguar E-Type 1961-1966
Jaguar E-Type 1966-1971
Jaguar E-Type 1971-1975
Jaguar XKE Collection No. 1
Jaguar XJ6 1968-1972
Jaguar XJ6 1973-1980
Jaguar XJ12 1972-1980
Jaguar XJS 1975-1980
Jensen Cars 1946-1967
Jensen Cars 1967-1979
Jensen Interceptor 1966-1976
Jensen-Healey 1972-1976
Lamborghini Cars 1964-1970
Lamborghini Cars 1970-1975
Lamborghini Countach Collection No. 1

Land Rover 1948-1973
Land Rover 1958-1983
Lotus Cortina 1963-1970
Lotus Elan 1962-1973
Lotus Elan Collection No. 1
Lotus Elan Collection No. 2
Lotus Elite 1957-1964
Lotus Elite & Eclat 1975-1981
Lotus Esprit 1974-1981
Lotus Europa 1966-1975
Lotus Europa Collection No. 1
Lotus Seven 1957-1980
Lotus Seven Collection No. 1
Maserati 1965-1970
Maserati 1970-1975
Mazda RX-7 Collection No. 1
Mercedes Benz Cars 1949-1954
Mercedes Benz Cars 1954-1957
Mercedes Benz Cars 1957-1961
Mercedes Benz Competition Cars 1950-1957
MG Cars in the Thirties
MG Cars 1929-1934
MG Cars 1935-1940
MG Cars 1948-1951
MG TC 1945-1949
MG TD 1949-1953
MG TF 1953-1955
MG CARS 1952-1954
MG Cars 1955-1957
MG Cars 1957-1959
MG Cars 1959-1962
MG Midget 1961-1979
MG MGA 1955-1962
MGA Collection No. 1
MG MGB 1962-1970
MG MGB 1970-1980
MG MGB GT 1965-1980
Mini-Cooper 1961-1971
Morgan Cars 1936-1960
Morgan Cars 1960-1970
Morgan Cars 1969-1979
Morris Minor 1949-1970
Morris Minor Collection No. 1
Nash Metropolitan 1954-1961
Opel GT 1968-1973
Packard Cars 1920-1942
Pantera 1970-1973
Pantera & Mangusta 1969-1974
Pontiac GTO 1964-1970
Pontiac Firebird 1967-1973
Porsche Cars 1952-1956
Porsche Cars 1960-1964
Porsche Cars 1964-1968
Porsche Cars 1968-1972
Porsche Cars in the Sixties
Porsche Cars 1972-1975
Porsche 911 Collection No. 1
Porsche 911 Collection No. 2
Porsche 914 1969-1975
Porsche 924 1975-1981
Porsche 928 Collection No. 1
Porsche Turbo Collection No. 1
Reliant Scimitar 1964-1982
Riley Cars 1945-1950
Riley Cars 1950-1955
Rolls Royce Cars 1930-1935
Rolls Royce Cars 1940-1950
Rolls Royce Silver Cloud 1955-1965
Rolls Royce Silver Shadow 1965-1980
Range Rover 1970-1981
Rover 3 & 3.5 Litre 1958-1973
Rover P4 1949-1959
Rover P4 1955-1964
Rover 2000 + 2200 1963-1977
Saab Sonett Collection No. 1
Singer Sports Cars 1933-1954
Studebaker Cars 1923-1939
Sunbeam Alpine & Tiger 1959-1967
Triumph Spitfire 1962-1980
Triumph Stag 1970-1980
Triumph TR2 & TR3 1952-1960
Triumph TR4 & TR5 1961-1969
Triumph TR6 1969-1976
Triumph TR7 & TR8 1975-1981
Triumph GT6 1966-1974
Triumph Vitesse & Herald 1959-1971
TVR 1960-1980
Volkswagen Cars 1936-1956
VW Beetle 1956-1977
VW Karmann Ghia Collection No. 1
VW Scirocco 1974-1981
Volvo 1800 1960-1973
Volvo 120 Series 1956-1970

CONTENTS

ACKNOWLEDGEMENTS

This is the second in a triology of Brooklands titles covering the post war 'T' series Midgets the TC, TD and TFs.

With peace coming to Europe in 1945 the MG management at Abingdon turned once again to sports car prodution and introduced the TC Midget in October of that year. It was a time when Britain badly needed revenue from exports so MG headed west and prised open the door to the US market. The result was that one in five of the 10,000 TCs manufactured crossed the Atlantic.

By 1949 the TC was looking dated, most of its design went back to the TA of 1936 and something more sophisticated was needed to take the marque into the fifties.

The TD went into production in November 1949 and its development and progress can be traced through the pages that follow. It was a great success nearly 30,000 were built before the TF came on stream in 1953 and of these over 80% were exported, the majority going to North America.

Brooklands Books are a reference series for enthusiasts, they are printed in small numbers and cater to the needs of owners of older interesting cars. The articles that appear in them are copyright and could not be reproduced without the co-operation and understanding of the publishers of the world's leading automobile journals. We are indebted to the management of Auto, Autocar, Autosport, Cars & Car Conversions, Light Car, Modern Motor, Motor, Road & Track, Speed Age, Sports Car World and Thoroughbred & Classic Cars for their ongoing help and support.

The handsomely restored 1953 TD on the cover belongs to Maurice Jackson of Burnham-on-Sea who graciously photographed NNE 875 for us all to enjoy.

R.M. Clarke

Coil Springs for the M.G. Midget

Extra Comfort and Controllability Offered by the Series TD Two-seater

COURAGE of a high order is needed to change a car which has been successful, and especially to change a car which has been uniquely able to charm owners in distant markets, such as the U.S.A. Nevertheless, the directors of the M.G. Car Co., Ltd., have now decided that the Series TC Midget, having put the sports car in fashion in North America, must henceforth give place to a successor of more modern design.

It is impossible to change a popular model without some regrets being aroused, as was evident in 1936 when the first of the present style of push-rod o.h.v. M.G. Midget engines superseded overhead-camshaft models. But, just as experience showed that the more flexible and refined modern engine could be tuned as successfully as was its predecessor, so it cannot be doubted that the latest M.G. Midget will quickly prove itself to be an all-round improvement over its slightly lighter predecessors.

In essential character there has been no change, the Midget remaining a vivacious open two-seater for those sufficiently young in spirit to find fun in fresh-air motoring. There has been no move towards the fashionable full-width style of coachwork, either, for somehow there is far more incentive to really keen driving in the older sort of sports car with front wings clearly visible on either side of a long, low bonnet. What has happened is that the car has been given an infusion of the most modern ideas on chassis design, which promises to make the Midget a comfortable riding car, and also an even more controllable one than ever before.

Closely akin to that used in the TC series cars, the TD series power unit is, in fact, substantially identical to that which has recently been fitted to open tourer versions of the four-seater 1¼-litre model. The four cylinders, of stroke/bore ratio 1.35/1, have Aerolite

M.G. MIDGET (Series TD) DATA

Engine Dimensions :			Chassis Details :		
Cylinders	..	4	Brakes ..	..	Lockheed hydraulic (2L.S. front)
Bore	..	66.5 mm.			9 ins.
Stroke	..	90 mm.	Brake drum diameter		99.5 sq. ins.
Cubic capacity	..	1,250 c.c.	Friction lining area ..		
Piston area	..	21.6 sq. ins.	Suspension :		
Valves	..	Pushrod o.h.v.	Front ..	..	Coil and unequal wish-
Compression ratio	..	7.25 to 1			bone I.F.S.
			Rear	..	Semi-elliptic leaf
Engine Performance :			Shock absorbers	..	Luvax-Girling
Max. power	..	4.4 b.h.p.	Wheel type	..	Steel disc
at		5,200 r.p.m.	Tyre size	..	5.50 × 15 ins., Dunlop
Max. b.m.e.p. ..		126 lb./sq. in.	Steering gear ..		Rack and pinion
at		2,600 r.p.m.	Steering wheel	..	16½ ins. dia., spring spoke
B.h.p. per sq. in. piston					
area	..	2.52	Dimensions :		
Piston speed at max.			Wheelbase	..	7 ft. 10 ins.
b.h.p., ft. per min. ..		3,070	Track ..	..	
			Front	..	3 ft. 11¾ ins.
Engine Details :			Rear	..	4 ft. 2 ins.
Carburetter	..	Twin S.U. inclined	Overall length	..	12 ft. 1 in.
Ignition ..	..	12-volt coil	Overall width ..		4 ft. 10⅝ ins.
Plugs : make and type		14 mm.: Champion L1OS	Overall height:		
Fuel pump	..	S.U. electric	Hood up ..		4 ft. 5 ins.
Fuel capacity	..	11 gallons	Screen down	..	3 ft. 9 ins.
Oil filter	..	Full-flow	Ground clearance	..	6 ins.
Oil capacity	..	9 pints	Turning circle	..	31¼ ft.
Cooling system	..	Pump and fan	Dry weight ..	..	17¼ cwt.
Water capacity	..	12 pints			
Electrical system	..	12-volt Lucas	Performance Data :		
Battery capacity	..	51 amp.-hr. at 10 hr. rate	Piston area, sq. ins.		
			per ton ..	..	25
Transmission :			Brake lining area, sq.		
Clutch ..	..	Borg and Beck 7¼" s.d.p.	ins. per ton ..	..	115
Gear ratios :			Top gear m.p.h. per		
Top	..	5.125	1,000 r.p.m.	..	14.5
3rd	..	7.098	Top gear m.p.h. at		
2nd	..	10.61	2,500 ft./min. piston		
1st	..	17.94	speed ..	..	61.2
Rev.	..	17.94	Litres per ton-mile,		
Prop. shaft	..	Hardy Spicer, open	dry ..	..	3,000
Final drive	..	Hypoid bevel			

alloy pistons carrying three rings apiece, and the combustion chambers of the cylinder head carry overhead valves of unequal size; inlet valves of 30 mm. throat diameter give good breathing, while exhaust valves of 4 mm. smaller size are more readily cooled.

Dual S.U. carburetters of 1¼-in. size, with downwardly inclined choke tubes, and dual springs for the overhead valves are further engine details contributing to the attainment of 54.4 b.h.p. output at 5,200 r.p.m., stamina being looked after by the sturdy, counterbalanced, three-bearing crankshaft.

One of the most attractive features of the TC Midget was the gearbox, and although a newer design has been adopted for the TD, with very slightly wider spacing of the ratios to suit a small increase in car weight, it is a design which is already known to respond well to sporting quick-change techniques. An orthodox sports-car remote control is used, bringing a short and sturdy

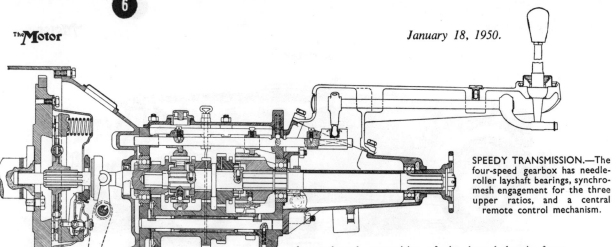

SPEEDY TRANSMISSION.—The four-speed gearbox has needle-roller layshaft bearings, synchro-mesh engagement for the three upper ratios, and a central remote control mechanism.

gear lever to a convenient central position near the steering-wheel rim.

A short, open propeller shaft, well suited to smooth running up to very high speeds, transmits power from the gearbox to a wide-track rear axle. This unit is of new design and incorporates sturdy hypoid-bevel gears which offset the pinion shaft 1 in. below the level of the axle shafts. The final-drive ratio is identical on TC and TD series cars, but the new 5.50-15 size tyres are of smaller effective diameter than the narrower-section tyres on larger-diameter wheels hitherto employed.

Stiff Frame, flexible Springs

Apart from the gain in comfort which use of E.L.P. tyres would provide, there is a completely fresh design of chassis frame and springing, taking full advantage of experience gained with the 1¼-litre model, but especially adapted to the requirements of a two-seater sports car.

The actual chassis frame comprises two box-section side rails extending the full length of the car, linked by tubular and other cross-members, and also bridged by a tubular arch member at the scuttle, which would greatly protect the passengers in the event of a crash. At the front, the dashboard structure is employed to stiffen the chassis, and the radiator is braced to this structure also, no effort having been spared to give this open-car frame the stiffness normally associated with designs reinforced by steel saloon coachwork. The frame side rails are sharply upswept at the rear to pass over the axle beam, and although the car is generally low built it has an amount of ground clearance which should allow negotiation of extremely rough tracks without damage. This generous ground clearance in vital places, coupled with wide-section tyres and a slightly rearward weight distribution, should make the TD series cars very attractive to enthusiasts for trials.

Although an experimental series of racing single-seater M.G.s was built with independent wheel springing many years ago, this is the first sports Midget to be so equipped, the layout chosen being one designed to give precise controllability and to require a minimum of maintenance. Each wheel is located by a pair of transverse wishbone members, the lower being longer than the upper to reduce variations in track with spring deflection, two widely spaced bearings threaded to retain lubricant forming the steering swivels.

The actual front springs are of coil type, acting between the lower wishbone member on each side and

the outboard extremities of the boxed-chassis front cross-member. Luvax Girling hydraulic shock absorbers, of generous size, are incorporated in the design, their arms forming the upper wishbone members of the I.F.S. linkage. Semi-elliptic seven-leaf rear springs are similarly damped, and have rubber inter-leaving to eliminate any possibility of squeaking in service.

Braking to suit the requirements of fast drivers is promised by the use of Lockheed hydraulic operating mechanism in 9-in. drums. The front brakes are of

COILED.—The TD model differs particularly in suspension details from earlier Midgets, as witness the coil spring and wishbone I.F.S. shown here.

two-leading-shoe type, giving a preponderance of front braking in normal driving, but the opposite effect when the car is being reversed, an arrangement ensuring utmost controllability at all times. The hand-brake control operates the rear shoes by a cable mechanism, and all brake drums are of cast iron, further reinforced by a single stiffening rib.

Probably the most precise known mechanism for the purpose, a rack-and-pinion gear is used for the steering and is set ahead of the front hubs to give a good rake to the steering column. This mechanism is self-adjusting for normal amounts of wear, and is linked to the stub-axle assemblies by a single drag link on each side of the car. The turning circle is compact at a fraction over 31-ft. diameter and the steering, geared at 2¾ turns from lock to lock, should remain extremely positive during the life of the car.

The coachbuilt body is essentially a two-seater, with accommodation for luggage as well as for the hood and

COMPLETE COVER.—
Protection against the
worst weather is pro-
vided when the neat
hood and side screens
are erected.

side screens behind the seats, and with optional provision for a further luggage rack above the external fuel tank. The spare-wheel carrier, set on a tubular framework behind the petrol tank, may be modified to carry a second spare wheel and tyre if this is needed for competition purposes.

Twelve-volt electrical equipment is standardized and the curved-fronted external head lamps may be supplemented by a fog lamp when required. The leathercloth-covered facia panel incorporates a glovebox on the passenger's side (dimensioned to accommodate a radio set if required) and a matched pair of 5-in. m.p.h. and r.p.m. indicators directly facing the driver, instrumentation being completed by an ammeter, oil-pressure gauge and clock. Indication of a low level of fuel in the 11-gallon tank is given by a flashing warning light.

Individual seat cushions may be adjusted for position, as may the shaped single-piece backrest, and a telescopic steering wheel with 3-in. adjustment range makes further provision for drivers of varying stature. The seats are upholstered in leather and a cover is provided for the folded hood, which latter, as may be seen from the photographs, is of neat contour when erected or drops completely out of sight into the body.

Modern items of equipment, such as bumpers and dual stop lamps, the extra-stiff frame needed with independent front-wheel suspension, and such contributions to stability as large-section tyres and wider-track axles, have inevitably made the M.G. Midget Series TD a rather heavier car than its predecessors. A

modest upward revision in the number of engine revolutions made per mile in top gear is stated, however, to have avoided any loss of acceleration, hill-climbing performance or speed, and the M.G. engine has proved so reliable in competitions and in ordinary service that it is unlikely to suffer from the resultant temptation towards the use of higher cruising r.p.m.

In its latest form, the M.G. Midget is likely to remain a popular favourite in many countries, and an 8 per cent. increase in the home price, to £445 plus purchase tax, is likely to be more than justified by the new refinements incorporated in the latest design.

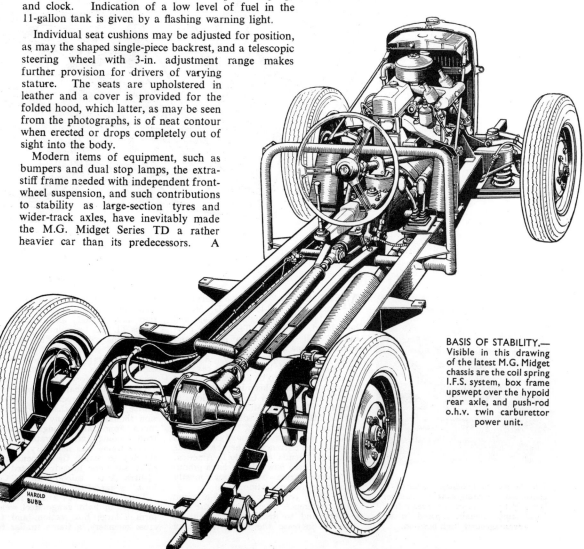

BASIS OF STABILITY.—
Visible in this drawing
of the latest M.G. Midget
chassis are the coil spring
I.F.S. system, box frame
upswept over the hypoid
rear axle, and push-rod
o.h.v. twin carburettor
power unit.

HAROLD
BUBB.

M.G. Midget Redesigned

FAMOUS SMALL SPORTS CAR
APPEARS AS THE 1950 SERIES
TD, WITH INDEPENDENT FRONT
SUSPENSION, BOX SECTION
FRAME, WIDER BODY, AND
MANY DETAIL IMPROVEMENTS

Autocar

The honest to goodness radiator is continued. A straight-across bumper is provided with substantial over-riders. Head lamps remain exposed in an advantageously high position.

MEET the new "Midge." Everybody calls the well-loved M.G. Midget the Midge, so it might just as well be printed. The Series TD may be new, but it still looks like a Midge, and has not "gone all futuristic," for which many thanks, people will say. A sports car ought to *look* like a sports car, and its innards ought to be accessible so that fans can personally keep it in tune; they should not be hidden beneath billows of bent tin. The latest Midget is, however, a little fatter and more solid than before.

During recent years a swarm of Midgets has gone far round the world earning hard currency. They have made many new friends, especially in America, and from these new friends have gradually come various suggestions, mostly requesting modernization.

The M.G. team sat down to a round table conference to sift out all the suggestions and to decide what might be done to increase the attractiveness of

the Midget without spoiling its unique character. A prototype was made and rigorously tested, and from that the Series TD has been developed.

The first point was to improve the suspension, so that the lively car could maintain its performance over indifferent roads, and a higher degree of passenger comfort could be obtained. That entailed changing over to independent front suspension. It was, of course, imperative that a softer suspension should not in any way impair the much appreciated Midget qualities of road holding and accurate steering, so a new frame was necessary, and a new steering to match the suspension. The right solutions already existed on the 1¼-litre M.G. saloon—the "Comfort Fast" sister of the Midget.

Thus the TD has a new frame, side members of light gauge steel welded to form a large box section, and tubular cross members, a frame similar to that

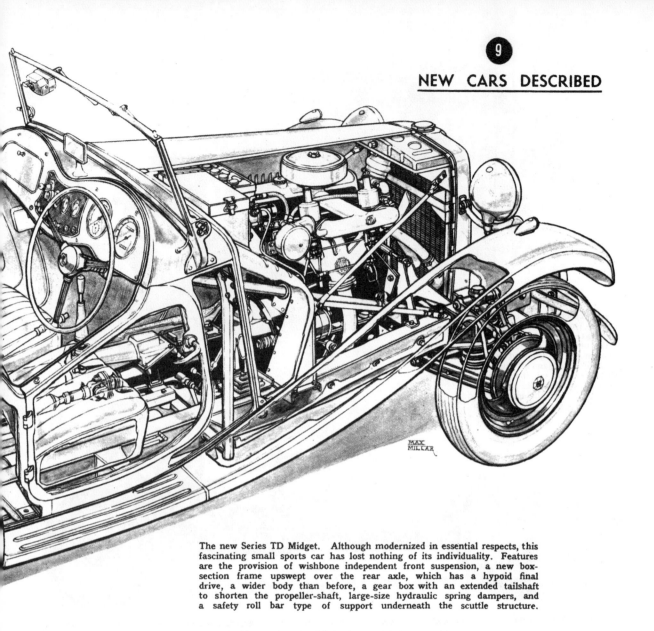

The new Series TD Midget. Although modernized in essential respects, this fascinating small sports car has lost nothing of its individuality. Features are the provision of wishbone independent front suspension, a new box-section frame upswept over the rear axle, which has a hypoid final drive, a wider body than before, a gear box with an extended tailshaft to shorten the propeller-shaft, large-size hydraulic spring dampers, and a safety roll bar type of support underneath the scuttle structure.

of the 1¼-litre except for one major point —the side members are not underslung beneath the rear axle, but are arched over the top of it, whereby the ground clearance is increased, an important point when softer suspension is operating over bad roads.

This new frame has a rather unusual provision. Across and above it in the region of the scuttle is welded a hoop of stout steel tube which has a double purpose. It adds support to the scuttle structure and steering column, and it provides protection for the occupants if the car should be overturned during some hectic trial.

Built into the front end of the frame side members is a downward arched cross member of large box section, which provides the mounting of the i.f.s. linkage. The system embraces the use on each side of a lower wishbone with its fulcrum anchored in rubber bushes to brackets beneath the cross member.

The wishbone is triangulated and the fulcrum points are spaced well apart in order to give longitudinal rigidity. To the apex of the wishbone is attached by means of a joint the lower bearing of the swivel pin. At the top of the swivel pin is a second bearing jointed to a tri-angular link which forms the upper wishbone and has its fulcrum in the main bearings of a double-piston hydraulic damper.

Two points of detail to note about this suspension system are that the swivel pin bearings are buttress screw threaded so as to provide a large area over which vertical thrust is spread, and the hydraulic dampers are the latest type of Luvax Girling with pistons of 1¼in diameter. Actual suspension is pro-vided by a low rate coil spring on each side, which is compressed between a housing formed in an extension of the front cross member and a pan built into the lower wishbone.

For the steering a direct-acting helical toothed rack and pinion gear is used, the ends of the rack being connected to the steering arms of the stub axles by jointed rods, so that steering and track-ing are performed by the same unit. The position of the joints is such that the rise and fall of the suspension does not affect the steering. This system again is similar to that used on the 1¼-litre saloon. The rear springs are laminated half-elliptics on rubber bushes, controlled by hydraulic dampers, and of a lower rate than formerly in order to conform with the i.f.s. Comfort is thereby increased.

It will be noticed that the familiar wire wheels have given place to disc wheels. There is a particular reason for this change. When this independent suspension system and the particular form of steering are used, the steering arms and links project rather far into the plane of the wheel, and to give the

One unexpected effect of the disc wheels from this angle is to emphasize the increase in width of the new M.G. (The track has been increased from 3ft 9in to 3ft 11⅜in front, and 4ft 2in rear). With the hood up, the Midget is beginning to look like a full-sized touring car, but photographs tend to exaggerate the size.

The sturdy design of the frame is revealed by this picture. Observe the roll bar structure which strengthens the scuttle when the body is mounted. The remote-control gear box is preserved.

Simple wishbone linkage of the M.G. i.f.s. The hydraulic dampers are of large size, 1⅛in bore. Thrust on the king pins is taken by screw-threaded bushes. Notice the direct coupling of the rack and pinion steering to the steering arms, and the pear-shaped rubber "stopper" against which the wishbone pan makes contact when approaching full spring compression. Right : The side members of the new box section frame are swept up over the rear axle instead of beneath it as on the 1¼-litre saloon. Final drive is by hypoid bevel.

necessary clearances a somewhat undesirable arrangement of wire spokes would be necessary. A dished disc wheel avoids these perplexities. The new disc wheels have large chromium plated nave plates, and the appearance is quite pleasing.

Since one of the main assets of the Midget is its capacity to cover the ground fast without a heavy consumption of fuel, it was considered that no change in the excellent existing power unit was necessary. The four-cylinder 1,250 c.c. overhead valve engine is continued practically without alteration. It is able to develop 54 b.h.p. The only change of note is the provision of a T-shaped air intake pipe to the two S.U. carburettors, drawing through a single oil bath air cleaner. Efficient air cleaning plus full flow oil filtration should preserve the engine in dust-laden climates.

The mounting of the power unit in the chassis is similar to that of the 1¼-litre. The front rests on a rubber pad, the tail of the gear box rests on twin rubber cushions, and a rubber buffer resists rebound movement. The engine is prevented from undue rocking movement by an adjustable tie fairly high in front. It has, therefore, a cushioned mounting, but one in which any excessive movement is prevented.

As before, a four-speed gear box with

a short remote central gear lever is provided. But the gear box is improved; it is more compact, and the shafts have roller bearings. The tail of the gear box extends farther than formerly in order to reduce the length of the propeller-shaft. The clutch operating mechanism is cable controlled in a manner insulating it from engine movement. Aft of the open propeller-shaft is another innovation, a hypoid bevel rear drive.

Last, but not least, in the mechanical specification is the adoption of the latest Lockheed two-leading-shoe hydraulic

One of the features of the engine of the M.G. TD is the T-shaped air intake to the two S.U. carburettors connecting to an oil bath air cleaner.

brakes with 9in drums. The hand brake lever is of the pull-up type, centrally situated, and provided with a press-button ratchet; that is to say, the brake lever does not stay in the "on" position unless the button is pressed.

Although the Midget has not departed from its familiar and attractive styling, from its honest radiator to the large fuel tank at its tail, the body has been modified to considerable advantage, giving extra room, and the car as a whole is four inches wider. This does not detract from the appearance; in fact, the general impression is of increased sturdiness. There is much more room and luggage space. The single seat squab is adjustable for angle. The body is an open two-seater, with steel panels and leather upholstery, and the windscreen can be folded flat forward. Detachable side

M.G. MIDGET SERIES TD SPECIFICATION

Engine.—4 cylinders, 66.5×90 mm, 1,250 c.c. Overhead valves operated by push rods. Three steel-backed main bearings. Pump and fan water circulation. Forced oil feed by gear pump; full-flow oil filtration. Twin S.U. semi-downdraught carburettors. Compression ratio, 7.25 to 1. Maximum b.h.p., 54.4 at 5,200 r.p.m. Piston speed at max. b.h.p., 3,068ft per min. H.P. per sq in of piston area, 2.5. Road speed at 2,500ft per min piston speed, 61.18 m.p.h.

Transmission.—Single-plate Borg and Beck clutch. 4-speed gear box. Overall gear ratios: Top 5.125, third 7.098, second 10.609, first 17.938 to 1. Hardy-Spicer open propeller-shaft. Hypoid bevel final drive.

Suspension.—Wishbone and coil spring independent front, half-elliptic rear. Luvax Girling hydraulic dampers.

Steering.—Helical toothed rack and pinion. Right or left hand. Column adjustable for reach.

Brakes.—Lockheed hydraulic, two-leading-shoe, in 9in drums. Cable operated hand brake on rear wheels with adjustment at central hand lever. Total friction area, 99.48 sq in.

Tyres and Wheels.—Dunlop 5.50×15in tyres. Bolt-on disc wheels.

Fuel System.—11-gallon rear tank. S.U. electric pump. Claimed fuel consumption 39 m.p.g. at steady 30 m.p.h. Maximum fuel economy 42 m.p.g. at steady 20 m.p.h.

Electrical Equipment.—Lucas 12-volt, with automatic advance and c.v.c. dynamo. Both head lamp beams dip. Twin stop and tail lamps, twin horns.

Main Dimensions.—Wheelbase, 7ft 10in (238.8cm); track, front, 3ft 11⅜in (120.3cm); rear, 4ft 2in (127.0cm); overall length, 12ft 1in (368.3cm); height, hood down, 3ft 9in (114.3cm); hood up, 4ft 5in (134.6cm); width, 4ft 10¾in (148.9cm). Ground clearance, 6in (15.24cm). Weight (chassis only) 1,155lb (519.75kg).

screens are provided. The spare wheel is mounted at the back of the fuel tank, which has a quick-release filler cap.

Another feature is a rearrangement of the instruments. As before, the scuttle has two rounded humps. On the face of that opposite the driver a 5in speedometer and 5in rev counter with clock are mounted. There is a central panel carrying the ammeter, oil gauge, light switches, dip switch, horn button and minor controls, and on the passenger's side is a locker fitted with a lid. Provision is made for extras such as an inbuilt radio, chromium-plated luggage rack, twin spare wheel carrier, 6-inch rear tyres and wheels for competition purposes, fog lamp with support bar, and badge bar.

The angle of the back squab of the front seats can be set to suit the driver, and can be locked by the clamping screw shown. The seat cushion is adjustable for leg reach.

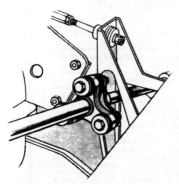

Flexible joint in the steering column of the M.G. Above it is the torque reaction tie for the engine mounting.

Functional style of the back of the car with the snap filler cap over the large tank, and the spare wheel, easy to reach. Two spare wheels can be had as an extra for competition purposes. In the latest arrangement of the instruments the speedometer and rev counter dials are in front of the driver, over the minor controls grouped in a central panel.

The Motor Road Test No. 1/50

Make: M.G. **Type:** TD Two-seater

Makers: The M.G. Car Co., Ltd., Abingdon-on-Thames

Dimensions and Seating

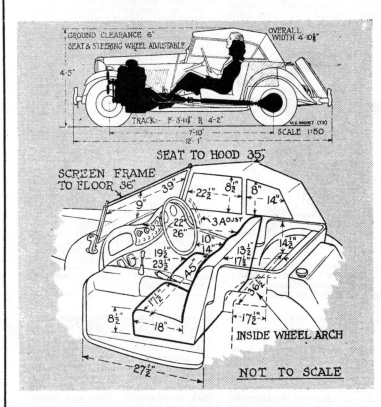

GROUND CLEARANCE 6"
SEAT & STEERING WHEEL ADJUSTABLE
OVERALL WIDTH 4'·10⅝"
4·5'
TRACK:- F 3·11⅜" R 4·2"
7'·10"
12'·1"
SCALE 1:50
M.G. MIDGET (TD)

SEAT TO HOOD 35"
SCREEN FRAME TO FLOOR 36"
NOT TO SCALE
INSIDE WHEEL ARCH

In Brief

Price £445 plus purchase tax £124 7 3 equals £569 7 3

Capacity	1,250 c.c.
Unladen kerb weight	18 cwt.
Fuel consumption	26.3 m.p.g.
Maximum speed	77.2 m.p.h.
Maximum speed on 1 in 20 gradient	63 m.p.h.
Maximum top gear gradient	1 in 10.6

Acceleration,
10-30 m.p.h. in top .. 11.5 secs.
0-50 m.p.h. through gears 13.5 secs.
Gearing, 14.5 m.p.h. in top at 1,000 r.p.m., 61.2 m.p.h. at 2,500 ft. per min. piston speed.

Specification

Engine

Cylinders	4
Bore	66.5 mm.
Stroke	90 mm.
Cubic capacity	1,250 c.c.
Piston area	21.6 sq. ins.
Valves	Pushrod o.h.v.
Compression ratio	7.25/1
Max. power	54.4 b.h.p.
at	5,200 r.p.m.
Piston speed at max. b.h.p.	3,070 ft. per min.
Carburetter	Twin S.U., inclined
Ignition	12-volt coil
Sparking plugs	14 mm. Champion L10S
Fuel pump	S.U. electric
Oil filter	Full-flow

Transmission

Clutch	Borg and Beck 7¼-in. s.d.p.
Top gear (s/m)	5.125
3rd gear (s/m)	7.098
2nd gear (s/m)	10.61
1st gear	17.94
Propeller shaft	Hardy Spicer, open
Final drive	Hypoid bevel

Chassis

Brakes	Lockheed hydraulic (2LS front)
Brake drum diameter	9 ins.
Friction lining area	99.5 sq. ins.
Suspension:	
Front	Independent; coil and unequal wishbones
Rear	Semi-elliptic
Shock absorbers	Luvax-Girling
Tyres	5.50 x 15-in. Dunlop

Steering

Steering gear	Rack and pinion
Turning circle	31¼ ft.
Turns of steering wheel, lock to lock	2⅜

Performance factors (at laden weight as tested)

Piston area, sq. in. per ton	20.6
Brake lining area, sq. in. per ton	94.9
Specific displacement, litres per ton-mile	2,420

Fully described in "The Motor," January 18, 1950.

Test Conditions

Fine, cold weather, with strong wind blowing along test stretch. Dry tarmac surface. British Pool petrol. Tests made with hood and sidescreens erected.

Test Data

ACCELERATION TIMES on Two Upper Ratios

	Top	3rd
10–30 m.p.h.	11.5 secs.	7.8 secs.
20–40 m.p.h.	11.8 secs.	7.7 secs.
30–50 m.p.h.	12.7 secs.	8.9 secs.
40–60 m.p.h.	17.3 secs.	—

ACCELERATION TIMES Through Gears

0–30 m.p.h.	5.5 secs.
0–40 m.p.h.	9.0 secs.
0–50 m.p.h.	13.5 secs.
0–60 m.p.h.	21.3 secs.
Standing quarter-mile	21.5 secs.

MAXIMUM SPEEDS

Flying Quarter-mile

Mean of four opposite runs	77.2 m.p.h.
Best time equals	82.6 m.p.h.

Speed in Gears

Max. speed in 3rd gear	61 m.p.h.
Max. speed in 2nd gear	41 m.p.h.
Max. speed in 1st gear	23 m.p.h.

FUEL CONSUMPTION

39.5 m.p.g. at constant 30 m.p.h.	
34.5 m.p.g. at constant 40 m.p.h.	
29.5 m.p.g. at constant 50 m.p.h.	
24.5 m.p.g. at constant 60 m.p.h.	
20.5 m.p.g. at constant 70 m.p.h.	

Overall consumption for 395 miles, 15 gallons, equals 26.3 m.p.g.

WEIGHT

Unladen kerb weight	18 cwt.
Front/rear weight distribution	49/51
Weight laden as tested	21 cwt.

INSTRUMENTS

Speedometer at 30 m.p.h.	5% fast
Speedometer at 60 m.p.h.	4% fast
Distance recorder	3% fast

HILL CLIMBING (at steady speeds)

Max. top-gear speed on 1 in 20	63 m.p.h.
Max. top-gear speed on 1 in 15	57 m.p.h.
Max. gradient on top gear	1 in 10.6 (Tapley 210 lb./ton)
Max. gradient on 3rd gear	1 in 7.1 (Tapley 310 lb./ton)
Max. gradient on 2nd gear	1 in 5.1 (Tapley 425 lb./ton)

BRAKES at 30 m.p.h.

0.96 g. retardation (=31.4 ft. stopping distance) with 85 lb. pedal pressure.
0.94 g. retardation (=32.1 ft. stopping distance) with 75 lb. pedal pressure.
0.71 g. retardation (=42.5 ft. stopping distance) with 50 lb. pedal pressure.
0.30 g. retardation (=100 ft. stopping distance) with 25 lb. pedal pressure.

Maintenance

Fuel tank: 12½ gallons (2½ gallons reserve light). **Sump:** 9 pints, S.A.E. 30. **Gearbox:** 1¼ pints, S.A.E. 90 Hypoid. **Rear axle and differential:** 1¾ pints, Hypoid S.A.E. 90. **Steering gear:** Hypoid S.A.E. 90. **Radiator:** 12 pints (two drain taps). **Chassis lubrication:** By grease gun every 500 miles to 11 points, and every 12,000 miles to one point (steering gearbox). **Ignition timing:** Points just breaking at T.D.C. engine stationary. **Spark plug gap:** 0.020 in. to 0.022 in. **Contact-breaker gap:** 0.010 in. to 0.012 in. **Valve timing:** Inlet opens 11 degrees B.T.D.C. Inlet closes 57 degrees A.B.D.C. Ex. opens 52 degrees B.B.D.C. Ex. closes 24 degrees A.T.D.C. **Tappet clearances (hot/cold):** Inlet, 0.019 in. (hot), 0.020 in. (cold). Exhaust, 0.019 in. (hot), 0.020 in. (cold). **Front-wheel toe-in:** Nil. **Camber angle:** 1 degree positive. **Castor angle:** 2 degrees. **Tyre pressures:** Front, 18 lb.; rear, 18 lb. **Brake fluid:** Lockheed Orange (Lockheed No. 5 Overseas). **Battery:** 12-volt. Positive earth return. 51 amp./hr. **Lamp bulbs:** 12-volt earth return. Headlamps (home), O/S, 36-watt, N/S 36/36-watt. Headlamps (export), both 36/36-watt. Sidelamps, 6-watt. Number plate, 6-watt (miniature). Stop and tail lamps, 6/24-watt. Panel lights, 2.2-watt. Warning lights, 0.5-watt.

Ref. B/13/50

The TD-type M.G. Two-seater

Latest Edition of Ever-popular Midget Offers
Greater Comfort and More Speed

CLOSE on 900 miles of varied motoring in the new TD-edition of the M.G. Midget leaves no doubt that as the M.G. Car Co., Ltd., progresses down the alphabet in type designations, so, also, it progresses upwards in the provision of those qualities which make the widest all-round appeal to motorists whose tastes lie in small open cars of above-average performance. This judgment is passed after ownership experience of two TA models and more than nodding acquaintance with the TB and TC types—not to mention affec-

READY FOR ANYTHING.—An experimental burst of acceleration on full steering lock reveals that soft springing does not imply excessive roll on corners.

tionate memories of earlier Midgets dating right back to the original M-type of 1929.

As readers who studied the description of the new model in our issue of January 18 last will be aware, the TD differs more from its immediate predecessor than any other models of the T family. Amongst the outstanding changes which have been made are the provision of an entirely new chassis with independent coil-type front suspension and side members which pass over the rear axle instead of being underslung as in previous models, together with a notable increase in track and body width, plus a changeover to broader tyres fitted to smaller wheels.

These alterations have naturally produced some increase in overall weight, although the actual difference is not perhaps so great as an inspection of the car might suggest. Comparing the weighbridge figures for the kerb weight for the TC model tested in 1947 with that of the TD which recently passed through our hands, one finds a step-up from 16½ cwt. to 18 cwt., the latter weight taken with approximately 6 gallons of petrol aboard. In view of the many queries we received as to the effect of this increase on performance, it seems appropriate to deal with this aspect first.

Comparing the two sets of test figures obtained, it is notable to find that, in acceleration, the TD and TC run very closely parallel but with the decimal points in all but two cases (and these not exceeding one fifth of a second) in favour of the new model. In maximum

speed, moreover, the TD type proved very definitely superior, despite a very strong wind blowing down the test course which produced a difference of 9-10 m.p.h. in the speeds obtained in opposite directions.

To quote the exact figures, the TC clocked a 72.9 m.p.h. mean with head and side screens erect compared with a 77.2 m.p.h. mean for the TD in similar trim. Fastest run in the TD was at 82.5 m.p.h., a figure admittedly favoured by the wind but significant as illustrating the ability of the engine to survive revving in top gear well beyond the peak speed when conditions allow. Actual engine revs. represented by this speed are 5,700 (6,000 r.p.m. on the rev. counter) compared with the 5,200 r.p.m. at which the engine reaches its peak output. The mean speed, it is interesting to note, coincides very closely with the peak revs. of the engine—a fact which suggests that, from a pure performance point of view, the new effective gearing provides optimum performance.

Geared for Liveliness

A word or two should be said at this point on this question of gearing, since the axle ratio of the TD is identical to that of the TC, and the difference in effective ratio results from a change of wheel and tyre size. The new 5.50 by 15-in. covers replacing the 4.50 by 19-in. tyres used on the old model lower the top-gear road speed at 1,000 r.p.m. from 15.5 m.p.h. to 14.5 m.p.h.

This automatically raises another query: does the TD seem undergeared?

To answer that question fairly, it is necessary to take into consideration the useage to which the car is put as well as the characteristics of the engine. So far as the former is concerned, there is no doubt that, for high-speed cruising on a typical Continental road, a higher axle ratio would be welcome. Against that, there would obviously be some loss in acceleration and hill climbing as well as in the notable flexibility which is an outstanding feature of the TD. It is noteworthy, moreover, that the engine shows a delightful willingness to rev. and that, although one is conscious that it is turning over at high speed when one is travelling quickly, the feeling is that of handling a piece of machinery which is built to run fast—and like it.

A cruising speed of 60 m.p.h. is easy to reach and maintain and one has no hesitation in making full use of 70 m.p.h. as and when conditions are appropriate. The speedometer fitted to the test car, incidentally, was less optimistic than most, with a maximum error of less than 5 per cent.

In the matter of petrol consumption, the extra weight and lower effective gearing of the new model does, of course, have some adverse effect, but the fact that the TD still records a figure on the right side of 20 m.p.g. at a constant 70 m.p.h. is highly satisfactory—as are the other figures obtained.

Before leaving the subject of performance, one or two other points should be mentioned—such as the surprising lack of pinking on Pool petrol, the almost entire absence of running-on, and the ability of the engine to reach very high revs. without signs of valve bounce appearing. Against these good qualities it must be recorded that the engine is by no means silent mechanically, although, as indicated earlier, the whole lively behaviour of the unit is such that a degree of mechanical noise does not seem inappropriate and is not therefore objectionable. When the throttle is opened wide, the

ACCENT ON ACCESSIBILITY. – Now fitted with an oilbath air filter, the familiar M.G. engine and its accessories are readily accessible to the keen owner-mechanic.

M.G. Road Test—Contd.

exhaust system emits a contented growl which likewise seems in keeping.

Less attractive on the test car was the flapping of the hood fabric when the latter was dry. This reference to the particular state of the fabric may seem curious, but the fact is that the material used shrank to drum-like tautness when wet and sagged appreciably when dry. It hardly seemed, in fact, consistent with the quality of the general finish and appointments, which otherwise impressed as being good.

To revert to mechanical matters, the gearbox, with its remote control placed just where the driver's left hand drops on to it naturally, proved entirely in keeping with the performance. The synchromesh mechanism on the three upper ratios provided not only sure and rapid changes of the touring type, but also raised no objections to the snatch operation favoured by competition drivers in special tests. The clutch, moreover, proved both smooth and very positive in engagement and showed no resentment at starts being made in second gear provided a little extra finesse was used with the throttle.

Smoother and Safer

From a comfort angle, the new chassis, with its wider track, i.f.s. and larger tyres, represents a very marked improvement. Gone entirely is the old sports car harshness, the ride now giving a combination of firmness and freedom from road shocks which closely approximates the ideal for a car of this type. This improvement is accompanied by a definite advance in general road holding and cornering, particularly noticeable when a ridged surface is encountered unexpectedly on a fast corner.

There is some measure of oversteer and some slight trace also of roll, but both are kept within rigid limits and the car can be driven very fast on winding roads with ease and certainty. Coupled with these qualities is a steering gear which is comparatively high geared, but effortless to use, so that, if the car does slide—and it does not do so without considerable provocation—correction is swift and certain. Some reaction is felt through the steering wheel, but this is never great enough to be objectionable and will, in fact, be welcomed by many drivers who prefer to "feel" the steering rather than to handle a car which is entirely unresponsive in this respect. The column is, incidentally, adjustable for length.

So far as brakes are concerned, little

need be said beyond the fact that they are in every way as good as the figures quoted in the data panel suggest and that the new horizontal position of the hand brake between the seats is much more accessible than the old whilst being equally powerful in operation. As before, a racing-type ratchet is fitted.

Whilst the new body closely resembles the old, the increase in width represents a great improvement, especially when the side screens are in position and driver and passenger are wearing winter clothing; in these conditions there is now no suspicion of cramping. The seats themselves are particularly comfortable, especially if the owner takes some trouble to adjust the position of the cushions and the angle of the squab (both can be varied) to his exact personal requirements. This adjustment is, admittedly, rather more troublesome than some, but the effect, once everything is right, well repays the few minutes required.

On the score of luggage accommodation, the Midget is by no means above criticism. The space provided is barely sufficient for the week-end impedimenta of two persons and quite inadequate for holiday purposes without recourse to an external grid (which is, incidentally, available as an extra). One cannot help feeling that extending the body rearward a few inches would represent a very popular alteration.

Apart from the point already made with regard to the fabric, the hood is of really excellent design, being very easy to erect and having rigid sidescreens which give almost saloon-like visibility.

The car also scores good marks on forward visibility through the fold-flat windscreen, but the choice of a mirror position on the scuttle is not a particularly happy one, since the mirror itself cancels out the advantage of being able to see the near side front wing, whilst its reflections are apt to be obscured by mud or mist on the rear window. Most users will feel that the old external position on the screen pillar is to be preferred.

Finally, a quick look round at details which have not so far been mentioned: The headlamps are adequate for a 60 m.p.h. cruising speed . . . the new position of the large-dial speedometer and rev. counter gives the driver a good view of the former, but results in the speedometer readings in the 50-70 range being somewhat obscure by the wheel rim . . . the horn button on the instrument panel can be operated without removing the left hand from the wheel, which represents an improvement on the conventional wheel-centre position, although it is a little foxing to strange drivers . . . the use of a warning light which flashes when the fuel level drops below a pre-determined point is excellent, but the choice of that level did not seem very happy, since the first flash occurred with well over 100 miles of motoring still in the tank and the light proved distinctly distracting at night . . . the size of the tank itself (12½ gallons) is excellent, but an improvement could be effected by swinging the quick-acting cap through 90 degrees to permit the user either to see into the tank or to use a dipstick . . . and details which called for whole-hearted approval included a rest for the driver's clutch foot, a handy tool locker under the bonnet (which, being of the side-opening type, gives first rate engine accessibility), an accessible battery position and the provision of sockets for an inspection lamp on the instrument panel.

In all, the TD proved to be a car which, like its forerunners, one took to with enthusiasm and parted from with reluctance, the only difference being that both the enthusiasm and the reluctance were greater than before.

SPEED FOR TWO.—Adjustments for steering wheel, cushions and backrest allow the driver to choose his ideal position in a car designed to carry two people and a modest amount of luggage.

The Tech. Ed. tries the new M.G.

TC vs. TD

BY JOHN R. BOND

In September 1936, the M.G. Car Company of Abingdon-on-Thames, England, announced a revised version of their popular small sports car—designated model T, first of the "T" series. At that time, certain revisions to the mechanical specifications caused howls of protest and anguish that could even be heard in America. Today, fourteen years later, the introduction of the fourth descendent of the "T" line, the long awaited TD model, has again provoked similar howls, but this time from both sides of the Atlantic.

In 1936, the cries came from the devout overhead cam worshippers who did not like the change to pushrod valve actuation. Today, the record of durability and performance set by the simpler type engine makes the early protests seem very foolish. Complaints regarding certain features of the new TD will be summarily disposed of later . . .

The 1950 M.G. Midget Model TD is essentially the same car as the TC with the following more important changes:

1. Left hand drive steering is available for the first time.

2. Independent front suspension with coil springs.

3. An entirely new frame.

4. 15″ bolt-on wheels with 5.50 tires.

5. Two leading shoe front brakes.

6. Rack and pinion steering gear.

7. A new hypoid rear axle.

8. Wider tread.

9. Moderate styling and "trim" revisions.

In the above list, the option of left hand driving position is long overdue for safe solo travel in this country. The change-over to independent front suspension, aside from many technical advantages, is an obvious attempt to soften American sales resistance thru the medium of softer springs, both front and rear. The stiffer frame is, of course, necessitated by the adoption of independent front suspension, while the new steering gear is another "overdue" improvement, the old worm being what is . . . or wasn't.

The new steering requires 2¾ turns from lock to lock whereas the TC took 1⅔ turns, but the new model turns much shorter so the change in ratio is more in the order of 2¼ on the TC to 2¾ on the TD.

Universal grouse regarding the TD concerns the "looks" with special comments directed to fenders and wheels. Apearance is strictly a matter of personal opinion or prejudice and if anyone wants to remove 6" from the leading edge of the front "wings" the job should be fairly simple for a good body and fender man.

The loss of the precious wire wheels is a low blow to the hard-shelled M.G. enthusiast. However, the writer feels that knock-off wire wheels can never be justified on *any* basis except "looks" for a moderate priced sports car. Compared to the conventional bolt-on steel disk, the wire wheel is definitely heavier (some 3 lbs. per wheel and tire assembly on the M.G.), certainly not as strong, harder to keep clean, and most important of all, much more expensive to manufacture and maintain. Disk wheels have been very successful on B.M.W. sports cars and on Indianapolis race cars. A final blow is the increased overhang and resultant unfavorable wheel bearing and spindle loading conditions required with wire wheels. Better brake cooling is an admitted advantage of the now obsolete wheel construction, but is of no importance for American road conditions. Quick wheel changing is of no importance, since it is so seldom required, and manipulating the jack takes more time than the actual wheel change even with five bolts instead of one big wing nut.

A brief road test was possible, made on the actual car shown in the accompanying photos, which had incidentally, only 200 miles on the odometer. Obviously, no performance runs against the watch were possible, but the ride and cornering characteristics were carefully observed. There is no question but that both of these important characteristics are much improved. The ride is noticeably more level, with none of the previous front end "bobbing constantly" or the rear end jar of the TC. Yet, the ride is definitely not soft by American standards and, consequently, the car rolls very little.

Cornering is much improved. Tire squeal does appear earlier, but the car seems to drift around turns in a manner much easier to control than the TC on which the front wheels seem to stick and the back end wants to come around rather too fast at times. There was no possibility of trying fast bends at really high speeds, but the softer independent front suspension and semi-elliptic rear springs should keep the lighter wheels and tires in more constant contact with the road surface with even more pronounced improvement under such conditions.

A complete performance analysis will appear in ROAD and TRACK for April. For a quick look, however, it may be noted that the TD is not only faster but, despite being 198 pounds heavier, it will get up to top speed more rapidly than the TC. Using rough figures, the TC clocks 78 mph maximum, corresponding to an engine speed of 4940

The new TD takes well to white-sidewall tires. Top has less peak and better lines. Good bumpers, now standard equipment, have long been a necessity for U. S. owners.

RPM. In other words, the older model is "geared" so that the engine cannot reach its peaking speed of 5200 on level roads in top gear. The new TD, with the same gear ratio of 5.125 to 1, but smaller wheels, will clock in the region of 82 mph corresponding to an engine speed of 5600 RPM, which is in accordance with modern practice as to gearing for optimum performance.

A complete analysis, including power to weight ratio, performance factors, horsepower required, horsepower available, effect of gear ratio changes etc., will appear in Part II of this article.

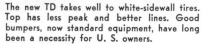

Sloping gas tank and spare tire along with built in tail lights, give new TD a clean "racy" look. Luggage rack is part of optional equipment.

The new TD incorporates many features of the 1¼ litre M.G. Tourer, shown below. Very similar are the frames, i.f.s., wheels, hardware, steering wheel and bumpers.

TC vs TD

by John Bond

Part II

In Part 1 of this article the new features incorporated in the M.G. Model TD were outlined, and a few impressions of a brief road test were recorded.

—PHOTO BY R. L. TRAMMEL

	TC	TD	TD
Axle Ratio	5.125	5.125	4.555
Engine Revs/Mi	3800	4100	3645
Cruising Speed	67	62	70
Apx. Top Speed	78	82	—
RPM @ Top Spd.	4940	5600	—
Max in 1st	25.7	23.0	25.9
Max. in 2nd	44.5	38.9	43.7
Max. in 3rd	64.4	58.1	65.4

In the above table, engine revolutions per mile for the TD are based on the use of American-built 5.50 x 15 tires with an average of 800 revolutions per mile. Cruising speed is based on the usual safe piston speed of 2500 feet per minute which on either the TC or TD engine (with 3.546 inch stroke) corresponds to 4240 RPM.

The additional top speed of the new TD model is difficult to explain satisfactorily. If we plot horsepower required to propel the two cars, as shown in Figure 1, against the published power curve, two things are apparent. One, the TC should do better than 78 mph, and two, the TD has a slightly more reserve power for acceleration or gradient.

Three different and unbiased British magazines give the top speed of the TC as under 80 mph, yet it seems reasonable to believe that given a sufficiently long or favorable stretch of level road, the TC might eventually reach a speed of nearly 85 mph. The theoretical top speed of any car is the intersection of power available with power required, as shown in Figure I. Note in this graph that at 75 mph, for example, the TC has 14 BHP in reserve to produce the acceleration required to increase speed, while the TD has 15 BHP in reserve. This explains why the TD has an apparently higher top speed—TD gearing makes the ultimate velocity more quickly and readily available.

Power required was calculated from the formula given in ROAD and TRACK January 1950, using a rolling resistance factor of 0.17, a wind resistance factor of .0017, test weights as previously given, and a frontal area for the TC of 16.5 square feet and 17.0 square feet for the TD.

Dealing now with the performance characteristics of the new M.G. Midget Model TD, as compared to the TC, the first point of concern is the net effect of the 198 pounds of added weight and the revised gear ratios.

The simplest method of calculating performance ability "through the gears" is on the basis of lbs./BHP and the following comparison speaks for itself:

	TC	TD
Curb Wt. (200 lb. load)	2011	2209
Lbs./BHP	37.0	40.6
Secs. 0-60 mph	22.7	23.3

As might be expected, the TD is slightly slower, though not as much as would have resulted if the gear ratios had not been revised slightly.

To properly evaluate top gear performance, the factor "litres of explosion volume per ton mile" can produce figures very close to actual results. This performance factor is simply:

Engine displacement in litres divided by engine revs/mile and multiplied by the displacement is equal to test weight in tons divided by two because the engine is a four-cycle type firing every other revolution.

Test weight (in the following comparison is taken as curb weight plus 200 pounds divided by 2240 to reduce the factor to "long tons" as used in England. American engineering departments use "cubic feet of explosion volume per U. S. ton mile" which is the same thing but in different units.

The revised gear ratios found on the new TD model have obviously been carefully contrived to offset the added weight. However, an optional axle ratio is available and it is interesting to note that whereas the TC gearing gives 3800 engine revolutions per car mile (or that RPM at 60 mph) the standard TD ratio requires 4100 revolutions to traverse a mile, and the optional axle ratio gives 3645 revolutions per mile. As the previous figures show, acceleration of the

TD, with standard axle ratio, through the gears is only fractionally slower than the TC and top gear acceleration definitely brisker. The following table gives a summary of the more important factors which can be compared:

	TC	TD
Axle Ratio	5.125	5.125
Litres/ton-mi.	2645	2600
Top gear acceleration: sec.		
10 to 30 mph	12.1	12.5
30 to 50 mph	14.9	12.9
10 to 50 mph	27.0	25.4

The effect of the gear ratio revisions on speeds in gears can be visualized from the following tabulation, all speeds given based on the recommended "peak" RPM. This value should not be confused with BHP "peaking speed" which is unchanged at 5200 RPM.

Figure I, below

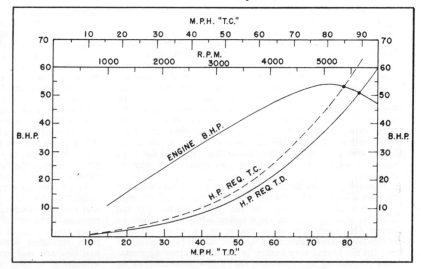

Cornering technique : Hilary Laing of the victorious British Ladies' Team in action in the slalom event, and the TD Midget on the climb to Val d'Isère.

WEEK-END ON

By GORDON WILKINS

Skis — and TDs

TWO OF THE NEW M.G. MIDGETS VISIT THE LOWLANDER SKIING CHAMPIONSHIPS AT VAL d'ISERE

SOME weeks before Christmas I was coming off the end of the Oxford by-pass when I saw in the distance an M.G. Midget with something unusual about its lines. I had heard that a new model was on the way and, as I was driving a very fast car at the time, I gave chase; but it was some time before I was able to catch it up, and to note that the family resemblance to other Midgets was now subtly modified by a general increase in size, the use of disc wheels and independent front suspension. Soon afterwards there came a 'phone call to know if I would like to take one out to Val d'Isère for a week-end in the French Alps, and I realized that it was over ten years since I had driven a Midget for any considerable distance. Like most enthusiasts, I drove and owned M.G.s of all kinds before the war, and a 2-litre convertible provided me with my first experience of covering 500 miles in a day in England.

However, export demands had kept production running at such a high level since the war that no radical changes had been introduced and the ten years' hiatus left me with no abiding sense of deprivation while there were so many new models of other makes to be tried. It was sufficient to know that thousands of happy youngsters in the United States were finding in the M.G. a new appreciation of motoring as a sport and that a new generation eking

out the bleak post-war years in England would give its ears for a chance to do likewise.

The idea was that we should take out two cars, one driven by Ian Appleyard, taking with him Louis Klementaski, the photographer, and the other driven by me with Bernard Till, a news-reel cameraman, as passenger. Appleyard, himself an Olympic skier, was taking out the trophy given by Viscountess Kemsley for the Lowlanders' Skiing Championships at Val d'Isère on January 14 and 15, and the two photographers were to cover the event and record the outward and homeward runs. The opportunity to try a new M.G. over a long distance was not to be missed on any account, but when combined with a chance of some skiing it seemed to present the prospect of an epic week-end. Moreover, my own skiing is not so good that I am above picking the brains of Olympic skiers when I get the chance. No false pride with me.

As an idea for a sporting week-end, the project sounded delightful, but the paperwork involved was considerable, and served to emphasize that the union of Western Europe remains a beautiful dream, which can take place only when the hordes of bureaucrats and assorted officials have been strangled with their own red tape. The car formalities are bad enough, but it is not until you have attempted to take a ciné cameraman as a passenger that

To make a film of one car, you need two, of course. The green car stops while the red Midget sweeps past on the snowbound mountain road near Bourg St. Maurice.

you know what delays and frustration can really mean.

Bernard Till's preparations had started weeks before. He had to get permission from his own union to work in France, and they had to apply for permission from the French Ciné Union for him to take films in France. His equipment, valued at £2,000, could not leave England until a Board of Trade export permit had been obtained. The procedure was so involved that shipping agents had to be employed and a full description down to the oilcan and the brush to flick the dust off the lenses had to be typed out twenty times.

Just before we left it was suggested that, as all his kit would be stacked in the Midget I was driving, I would need a permit from the French Ministry of Labour to act as a *chauffeur d'automobiles*, but this I nipped firmly in the bud.

Eventually everything was satisfactorily arranged—or so we thought. The two cars started from Trafalgar Square heavily laden with baggage and photographic equipment, and crossed on the Wednesday night ferry to Dunkirk. The plan was to take two days on the outward journey, taking films and still photographs en route and making a brief détour to Paris to pick up the ciné cameraman's permits. The brief détour quickly developed into a day of frantic interviews and telephone calls, and we found ourselves late on Thursday evening faced by a ruling from an apparently responsible official of the French Ministry of Labour that no film involving publicity for a British car must be made on French soil. However, promises of further consideration were given for the following day.

To continue the debate any longer would have meant abandoning the whole expedition, so we left the Champs Elysées for what we hoped would be a quick run to Fontainebleau and a good dinner to cheer us up. Immediately we ran into a thick fog which reduced us to a crawl the whole way and we were lucky to get an omelette before retiring to bed, fog-bound and frustrated.

We now had 400 miles to do on the Friday to get to Val d'Isère in time for the opening of the skiing championships on Saturday morning, and had to fit in such stops for still and ciné photographs as we could manage en route, whenever light and background were suitable. The cars were filled up with fuel and oil, and tyre pressures were increased from the recommended 18 lb per square inch to 21 lb. The run to Paris over the *pavé* of Northern France had already shown that this new Midget, with its fat tyres, independent suspension and strongly reinforced chassis frame, gave riding comfort far superior to that of its predecessors, but with the heavy loads we were carrying extra pressure seemed desirable to assist in holding a line on rough corners with an adverse camber. The increase proved to be exactly what was needed and from then on road holding was first-class at all speeds on wet *pavé*, snow or ice.

The fog was still with us and after 34 miles through the forest of Fontainebleau and on to Sens the speed never exceeded 60 m.p.h. From then on the weather cleared, the sun came out and we were really able to find out what the new Midget would do, as we sped down the long straights and open curves of N6. The roads were wet and slippery and the surface not always even, but the cruising speed could be maintained regardless of conditions.

Films and fresh air: The green car's crew take their air neat, while manœuvring into position for some 50 m.p.h. action studies.

The speed was pushed up until the car was holding a speedometer reading of 82½ m.p.h., and the rev counter needle was round to 5,500. A speedometer and rev counter calibration had already shown an optimism of about 8 per cent, but after making due allowance for this it was apparent that we were maintaining a cruising speed of 70-75 m.p.h. and confirmation soon came as we logged the times through Joigny, Auxerre, Avallon, and Saulieu to Arnay-le-Duc. The roads were wet, the traffic was fairly heavy by French standards and we were twice brought down to second gear in delays behind heavy lorries, but when we stopped for petrol at Arnay the 108.5 miles from Sens had been covered in 105 minutes, giving an average speed of 62 m.p.h.

The speed through the last section from Saulieu was reduced by preparations to film the petrol stop of the second car at Arnay and the average taken over the section from Sens to Saulieu was even better, with a distance of 91.5 miles covered in 87 minutes at an average of 63.1 m.p.h. The second car covered the stretch Fontainebleau to Avallon, 99.6 miles, in 98 minutes, averaging 61 m.p.h.

My car, which was the one used for *The Autocar* Road Test, had been run in the morning with head and side-screens erected but the sidescreen on the driver's side had been omitted. At the lunch stop at Chagny this screen was put into place and the complete enclosure of the car seemed to have an appreciable effect on speed. We are accustomed to the fact that closed cars are faster than open ones, but it looks as though the eddies caused by the absence of sidescreens may also have a measurable effect.

WEEK-END
on Skis – and TDs : continued

At all events, the car which had covered several flying kilometres in the morning in times between 29 and 30 sec now proved capable, heavily laden as it was with photographers' equipment, of spacing the kilometre posts at intervals of less than 29 sec, and covered one level stretch past an aerodrome in 28.4 sec, giving an average speed of 78.8 m.p.h.

As darkness fell there were signs that fog might cause further delays, so the route was switched through the Rhône valley over the high ground descending via Culoz to Aix-les-Bains. The lovely Lac du Bourget, which Balzac called " blue as no other in the world," was to us simply a darker patch in the surrounding night as we sped through the swerves of the Corniche. We stopped for dinner at Albertville and then started the long ascent from the rail-head at Bourg St. Maurice to Val d'Isère, where we arrived at midnight. This section of the road rises 6,050ft through a series of gorges and sharply ascending mountain roads and it was here on the snow and ice that the road holding qualities of the new Midget were appreciated to the full. By this time both crews were feeling tired, but the eager response and safe handling of the little cars made a pleasure of the difficult stretch, which could have been an ordeal in a less roadworthy car.

During the two days at Val d'Isère the weather was magnificent and we had the satisfaction of seeing the British team at the top of the combined results for downhill and slalom races. Two London sisters, Sheena and Vora Mackintosh, came first and second in the ladies' combined results and Hilary Laing was third. In the men's event John Boyagis, a young Briton who had the good fortune to be at school in Switzerland during the war, easily won the slalom. Count d'Ursel of Belgium returned such a magnificent time in the downhill race, flashing across the finishing line at about 60 m.p.h., that he won the cup for the best combined result. However, with Britons second, third and fourth, the team award was secured.

The Lowlander Championship is open only to residents in countries without mountains suitable for skiing, such as Britain, Belgium, Holland and Denmark, and entrants must not have ski-ed for more than 60 days in the previous winter. These qualifications apply to several competitions throughout the season, and give a chance to

Six thousand feet up, on the approaches of the Col d'Iseran, lies Val d'Isère, one of the highest resorts in France. The funicular takes skiers up another 2,400ft to the Tête de Solaise, from which a series of runs leads down to the village.

Although the Col d'Iseran is closed by snow from October until July, the road is kept open as far as Val d'Isère for the winter sports season.

January 27, 1950

the genuine holiday skier to take part in competitions with some hope of success.

Val d'Isère, as one of the highest French resorts, lying at 6,000ft at the foot of the Col d'Iseran, is assured of snow until the end of April. One funicular and two ski lifts are available and another funicular is in the course of construction. Hotel charges are moderate and skis can be hired for about £1 a week. Top quality skiing clothes cost from half to two-thirds of the prices now ruling in the West End

Towing the line : members of the British ski teams go skijoring behind one of the Midgets.

of London and first-class skis, which in Switzerland would now cost the equivalent of £20, can be bought for about £12 in French currency.

The need to conserve their holiday currency allowance has forced many British winter sports enthusiasts to buy their kit in England before they leave, but it is to be feared that they do not always receive the best advice, to judge by the pained expression worn by one 14-stone enthusiast, who was being told by his instructor that he had been sold a pair of lady's skis. Our two photographers, seeing the magic of the Alps in winter for the first time, realized at once why those who have once taken up skiing never again worry about a summer holiday, if only they can get away for a few days in the winter, and soon launched themselves on the perilous slopes. Bernard Till took the whole thing in his stride and indeed it must have been a tame affair to him, after filming bombing raids on Germany, operating as photographer with the Maquis, and always seeking excitement. Klementaski adopted a more cautious approach, but enjoyed himself immensely.

What with the British victories and the presence of a number of fellow motoring enthusiasts who were learning the mysteries of the skiing art, there was quite a party on the Sunday night. The frosty air and mountain liquors work powerfully upon those who normally partake but sparingly of strong waters and it has to be admitted that when the time came to rise for an early start on the Monday morning two members of the M.G. party were afflicted with that kind of full, imperial hangover, which is liable to develop into a complete fallover unless very great care is exercised when tying up the shoelaces. It should not be inferred from this that the title of this narrative must now be changed to "SKIS AND D.T.s," but the point is made because in the course of the long day's run from the Italian frontier right up to Dunkirk, the M.G.s earned our respect and gratitude as comfortable long-distance cars.

We started just before 8 a.m. as the first rays of the sun were setting the mountains aflame and the descent from Bourg to Chambéry was taken very gently. It is usually more difficult to descend than to ascend on snow or ice, and daylight revealed dizzy precipices over the unprotected roadside which had been mercifully hidden by darkness on the upward journey. Only 17 miles were covered in the

first hour and the second hour was little faster. Thereafter the speed improved, and the two cars kept together in convoy right across France. There were numerous stops for photographs and three stops for petrol, and we found time to dine off sole cooked in champagne at Rheims before embarking on the rough roads across the old battlefields to Dunkirk. The two cars had not followed exactly in each other's tracks, but by a strange coincidence, when they drew alongside the night ferry boat, both their trip indicators showed exactly 651.4 miles for the day's motoring. Checks on both cars against kilometre posts had shown an error of 3 per cent in the mileage recorders at the cruising speeds at which we were running and the correct mileage for the day was therefore 632.

It usually happens that on a trip of this length one changes drivers from time to time, but in this case I drove the whole distance single-handed, thus covering 1,000 kilometres in the day, and so I was in a position to speak with some appreciation of the comfort, driving ease, and general handiness of the Midget in long hours at fairly high speeds.

The two cars were among the earliest of the new type to be made and in the course of the week-end we encountered various minor difficulties, including some electrical troubles and a broken oil pipe—troubles of a kind which so often happen on the first samples of a new model—but they did not prevent our completing the run to schedule. The TD Midget undoubtedly represents a great advance over earlier models in steering, braking, road holding and riding comfort. Despite the extra weight entailed by the new amenities, the car is obviously able to maintain high averages for long distances with minimum fatigue to the occupants.

The axle ratio of 5.125 to 1 confers unusual top gear flexibility and scarcely any pinking was experienced even on French petrol. This will probably enhance the appeal in the American market, but it means that third gear, with its comfortable maximum of about 50 m.p.h., is little used except when accelerating or climbing steep hills. European users who expect to drive fast for long distances will probably be happier with the alternative axle ratio of 4.55 to 1 and should find it worth while to specify the optional double hydraulic spring dampers for bad roads. Over the whole trip fuel consumption on one car worked out at 24½ m.p.g. and the other showed approximately 23 m.p.g.

AUTOSPORT Road Test

*FAST COMPANY: The Mark II TD M.G.
at speed. It is capable of 90 m.p.h.*

The M.G. TD Midget Mark II

NOTHING has ever caused so much discussion among enthusiasts as the introduction of the "TD". To begin with, the general impression that the car was less sporting than its predecessors gained ground. It was argued that it had a wider body, was slightly heavier, had disc wheels, and independent front suspension. There is no doubt that many M.G. owners thought that their pet make had been spoilt.

It was with great surprise that the same enthusiasts saw "TDs" beating "TCs", round circuits, up and down Alps, or wherever motoring competitions were going on. Furthermore, they were vastly intrigued when M.G.s, instead of deploring the "hotting up" of their engines, actually sold "tuning" over the counter. The 1,250 c.c. push-rod o.h.v. power unit has long had a reputation for being unbreakable, and the makers certainly showed their faith in its ruggedness when they gave their blessing to this treatment.

The car I took over for test was a Mark II model; that is to say that it

had undergone modification from the basic specification to make it more suitable for high speed work. It is of interest that the M.G.s raced in this year's production car events were identical to the one I tried, and of course enough have been sold to qualify the type as standard.

The engine has bigger carburetters, and also larger valves, which are used in conjunction with a compression ratio of 9.2 to 1. Twin pumps ensure adequate fuel supply, and large air scoops are fitted to the front brakes. Small Andrex shock absorbers, set fairly slack, are employed in addition to the Girling hydraulic dampers.

Naturally, these improvements increase the price of the car, which works out as follows:—

List price of TD	£445	0	0
Purchase Tax	124	7	3
Mark II specification	50	0	0
Purchase Tax	13	17	10
	£633	5	1

So, even thus augmented, the outlay is moderate, and represents quite remarkable value.

After all the discussion that has taken place, I feel that many readers will want a direct comparison with older M.G.s, and luckily I have driven practically every model that has been turned out. I must admit that the suspension and steering of some of these did not appeal to me, and it is in those departments that the new series shows such a great advance. It is, in fact, much more comfortable than any previous M.G., and this has been achieved simultaneously with considerable progress in the roadholding department.

Good Springing

The springing is very good, and one is never conscious that it is working hard, even over bad roads. The heavy, box-section frame, with tubular cross members, is very rigid, and no doubt contributes largely to the good roadholding. No road shocks reach the steering wheel

SPECIFICATION and PERFORMANCE
DATA

Car Tested—M.G. Midget, Series "TD", Mark II, price including P.T. £633 5s. 1d. (see text).

Engine—4-cylinders, 66.5 m.m. × 90 m.m. (1,250 c.c.). Push-rod operated overhead valves. 9.2 to 1 compression ratio. Twin S.U. carburetters. Coil and distributor with automatic advance.

Transmission—Single plate clutch, 4-speed gearbox with remote control, ratios 1, 1.385, 2.07, and 3.50 to 1. Open propellor shaft. Hypoid bevel, semi-floating, rear axle, ratio 4.875 to 1.

Chassis—Box-section, with tubular cross members, carried over axle at rear. Independent front suspension, with wishbone links and helical springs. Semi-elliptic rear springs. Hydraulic and friction dampers, both at front and rear. Steel disc wheels with five-stud fixing, fitted 5.50 in. × 15 in. tyres. Lockheed hydraulic brakes, 2 L.S. in front, with 9 in. drums.

Equipment—12 volt lighting and starting. Speedometer, revolution counter, water temperature, oil temperature, and oil pressure gauges, ammeter, fuel warning light.

Dimensions, etc.—Wheelbase, 7 ft. 10 in. Track: front 3 ft. 11 3/8 in., rear 4 ft. 2 in. Overall length, 12 ft. 1 in. Turning circle, 29 ft. Weight as tested, 18½ cwt.

Performance—Maximum speed, 88 m.p.h. Speeds in gears, 3rd 60 m.p.h., 2nd 42 m.p.h. Acceleration, standing quarter-mile 20 1/10 secs., 0-50 m.p.h. 10 secs., 0.60 m.p.h. 15 secs.

Fuel Consumption—Driven hard, 28½ m.p.g.

been marred by the tuning operations, and one can potter along in top gear when in a lazy mood. The full performance of the car, however, is only available if one makes intelligent use of the gear lever. Given that type of handling, the lively little engine does not seem to notice the fairly considerable weight of the vehicle at all.

Easy Change Gearbox

The gearbox has an easy change, and is quiet on the indirect ratios. Third speed, in fact, is inaudible, and is consequently very pleasant as a traffic gear. Straight through changes present no difficulty, and the pedals are well placed for the "heel-and-toe" change down.

The Lockheed hydraulic brakes, with two leading shoes in front, are powerful, progressive, and do not fade. The mudguard design provides ample air for cooling, and scoops on the back plates assist the pierced disc wheels to circulate it over the drums. It is needless to remark that the well known "fly off" hand brake has been retained.

Plenty of luggage space is provided in the two-seater body, and a large glove box or cubby hole is positioned in the facia. For touring, an external

CONTINUED ON PAGE 89

OFFICE: A pleasant feature of this M.G. is the fully-equipped and well thought-out facia panel.

through the rack and pinion mechanism.

Violent cornering produces some roll, but this is not excessive. It is rather surprising that there is a slight over-steering tendency, which shows itself when one attempts to drift a bend. On the other hand, this makes the machine exceptionally easy to throw about, rendering it particularly suitable for such things as rally tests.

The little engine revels in hard work, and it seems impossible to over-drive it. Valve bounce begins at 6,200 r.p.m., but one can hold 6,000 r.p.m. indefinitely without causing any distress. At full bore, it naturally sounds "busy", but part throttle cruising in the seventies is a remarkably quiet and effortless proceeding, and is one of the most attractive qualities of the car. The flexibility of the unit has in no wise

POWER-HOUSE: Only visible alterations from the Mark I are the large-bore S.U. carburetters and dual electric fuel pumps. The engine displays a healthy appetite for high r.p.m.

ROAD and TRACK ROAD TEST No. F-3-51

Make: MG **Model: TD Midget**

HEIGHT 53"

CLEARANCE 6"

TREAD 47.3"
REAR 50"

WHEELBASE 94"

Price: $1850 f.o.b. U. S. Ports
Horsepower: 54.4 at 5200 rpm
Displacement: 76 cu in (1250 cc)
Bore: 2.56 in.
Stroke: 3.54 in.

Weight: 2016 lbs
Overall length: 145 in.
Overall width: 58-5/8 in.
Front seat width: Individual
Rear seat width: none
Tire size: 5.50x15

Third of a series of road tests of foreign and American automobiles from the American driver's viewpoint

Altho considerable roll is evident, the cornering ability of the MG is remarkably good.

Mr. X Reports on MG TD Road Test

"TC vs. TD" . . . this classic argument has greatly flavored MG TD road tests appearing in British publications. Performance, appearance, and design were either better than, or not equal to, the TC. This can be confusing to the person who has never driven the TC *and* the TD. Since I have never driven a TC-type MG, I can present an unbiased report on the TD.

The MG is like a tail-wagging dog, it seems to be anxious to make friends! After one settles into the individually shaped seats, a feeling of genuine comfort (like the old fireside easy chair) is obtained. The rake of the large diameter steering wheel, the man-sized tachometer and speedometer, the elbow-clearing cut of the door . . . all these create a sense of action. And, somehow, the proudly exposed headlights (of exceptional power) and the long center-hinged hood, becrowned with an honest-to-God radiator cap, proclaim an almost-forgotten masculinity. Here is a car to *go*, to ride like a *real* cowpuncher does a strawberry roan . . . to hell with aerodynamic jet-plane-inspired nightmares.

Thru the four nicely-selected gear ratios gives brisk acceleration to the accompaniment of a cocky exhaust crackle. Almost perfect is the stubby shift-lever perched atop the drive shaft tunnel . . . almost, because the 1st gear position is slightly awkward, and one *can* get into the reverse "blind alley" when making a fast 2nd to 3rd change. Clutch action is positive, quick, and without a trace of chatter even when abused. Altho somewhat crowded for big feet, the pedals are convenient and easy to accustom oneself to . . . particularly the roller-type accelerator.

Having witnessed the see-saw antics of TC drivers in a tight parking space, the short turning radius of the TD was a surprise. By taking advantage of the telescopic adjustment on the steering wheel, a very comfortable position was found. Positive control, a result of rack-and-pinion steering, made driving a real pleasure. The quick ratio gives 2¾ turns from lock to lock . . . almost half the turns required on the average American car. The only disadvantage to this is, that one tends to drive the car much harder than average because it is so much fun! The impossible becomes practical.

Forearmed with a feeling of security (watching MGs at road races does that) the TD was literally thrown around a twisting mountain pass. Once the adhesive limit was found, corners were taken in slides .. good slides, bad slides, and wild hairy slides. The control was so good that the white center line was never crossed until we finally "spun out." Altho the rear end does tend to "come-around" on fast turns, correction is both quick and positive. During such maneuvers, a moderate amount of roll can be obtained, but it is not accompanied by any degree of nose-dive unless brakes are being applied. (tsk, tsk!)

Having read an interesting "debate" in the British *Motor* in which Technical Editor Joseph Lowry claimed the MG TD possessed slight "oversteer" and the MG factory said it definitely had understeer, I was pleased to find no trace of either . . . completely neutral. This is a good compromise as the vintage enthusiasts favor oversteer while the modern school calls for understeer.

Two-way runs were made over a carefully measured quarter-mile course; stop watch readings were 79.2 mph upwind, and 82.8 mph downwind, for an average of 81.0 mph. At this speed the engine was particularly noisy, but gave no complaint at over 6,000 on the tach. Steering was good at this speed but the shaking of the cowl as well as high piston speeds of the engine, would make driving at this speed in anything but a race rather uncomfortable. At the normal cruising speed of 61 mph (at 2500 fpm piston speed) the engine and ride is completely smooth and one feels complete confidence in the car.

Were I the lucky owner of a TD, I would move the horn button - dip switch to an under-rim position at the left (export left-hand steering) and add a water-temperature gauge to the instrumentation. Instruments could also use improved lighting as the large lighted dials are distracting, yet unreadable at speed. Inconsistent with the general quality of the car was the top material—a pity for the TD is the type car which urges you to drive with the top down when possible. The design and location of the hand-brake are regrettable. When judged by the overall excellence of this exciting little car, these faults are minor indeed.

Mr. B Reports MG Road Test

Having most of my MG experience in TC models, my first impression of the TD was unfavorable; however, after approximately 100 miles of hard driving, the advantages of the TD overcame my partiality to the TC. At first, the somewhat higher seating position and the inability to see the right front fender proved somewhat disturbing. The most notable improvement over the TC is the use of rack and pinion steering which gives a positive feeling and accurate placement when cornering, impossible to obtain on the TC. In combination with the excellent coil sprung i.f.s. with unequal wishbones, this should more than offset the disadvantage (in road racing) of slightly heavier curb weight. Surprisingly enough, the acceleration proved equal to the TC... 0 to 50 mph in 13.0 seconds and the standing quarter-mile in 20.8 seconds. On our favorite test hill (32%), the TD, from a standing start, obtained a speed of 20 mph. This is equal to the performance of a 1951 Ford which has more than twice the hp rating of the MG. The MG, to date, has been the only car capable of backing up this hill at any point, due, of course, to its excellent weight distribution . . . 51% on the rear wheels.

As with all Nuffield products, the finish of the entire car was excellent. A useful amount of luggage can be stored behind the seat, a space which could in an emergency also accommodate small children or pets when the top is erected. The absence of a fuel gauge and water temperature gauge is regrettable, particularly in a sports car.

Since putting the TD thru its paces, I can easily see why the MG enjoys such a phenomenal popularity in this country.

MISCELLANEOUS SPECIFICATIONS

```
No. Cylinders . . . . . . . . . . . 4
Valve Arrangement . . . . pushrod ohv
Compression Ratio . . . . . 7.25:1
Carburetors . . . . . 2 S.U. inclined
Piston Speed at 5200 rpm  3,070 ft/min.
Ignition . . . . . . . . 12 volt, coil
Fuel Pump . . . . . . . S.U. electric
Spark Plugs . . 14 mm Champion L10S
Brakes . . . Lockheed hyd. (2LS front)
Brake Drum Dia. . . . . . . . 9 in.
Rear Axle Ratio . . . . . . . 5.125:1
```

The car for this test was furnished thru the courtesy of Gough Industries, of Los Angeles, distributors for MG and other Nuffield Products.

—COVER PHOTO BY J. JULIUS FANTA

The startling pictures above, and below, show the steep Fargo St. Hill, in Los Angeles. This 32% grade was no problem in the MG, as it easily climbed at 20 mph. Also, it was one of the few cars able to back up the hill successfully. Hill has been famous test spot for many years.

NEW M.G. FOR LE MANS
Streamlined Mark 2 TD for 24 Hours Race

Exclusive pictures of the businesslike M.G. which will be driven at Le Mans by entrant George Phillips and Alan Rippon. The car is essentially the catalogue Mark 2 TD chassis and the aerodynamic body owes much to experience with Lieut.-Col. Goldie Gardner's famous record-breaker. It is the first sports-racing car to be prepared at Abingdon for many years.

BRITISH ACHIEVEMENT

GOLDIE GARDNER DOES IT AGAIN IN UTAH WITH THE RECORD M.G.

The little record-breaker is towed out on to the dazzling salt flats. ("Motor Trend" photograph.)

This front view shows the smoothness of the enveloping body. Right: The American TD M.G. which captured at the same time 23 American records, at dawn on the flats.

A LTHOUGH the full programme of record attempts could not be carried out, Lt. Col. A. T. G. Gardner's recent capture of six international and ten American records in Class F with his famous record-breaking M.G. was a notable performance in several respects. For the first time, the engine used in the car was a development of the standard 1½-litre power unit, using the standard crankshaft and bearings, fitted with a Shorrock supercharger; and the results

obtained speak volumes for the durability and robustness of this unit.

The power output of the engine was raised to 92 b.h.p. for the longer distance records, which were the first attempted; it had been hoped to carry on for up to two hours, but a broken oil pipe forced a premature stop. Later, the compression ratio and supercharger pressure of the engine were raised to bring the power developed up to the altogether remarkable figure of 210 b.h.p. at 7,000 r.p.m.; with the engine in this form, records over short distances such as the flying mile and kilometre were to be attacked, but unfortu-

nately a breakdown in the timing apparatus delayed matters considerably, and by the time this had been rectified the weather had deteriorated and the track was too waterlogged to permit the attempt to be carried out. Consequently, this part of the programme had to be abandoned. Those records actually captured were (subject to official confirmation) as follows:—

INTERNATIONAL CLASS F (1,100 c.c. to 1,500 c.c.)	NEW RECORD	OLD RECORD
50 kilometres	127.8 m.p.h.	125.92 m.p.h
50 miles ...	130.6 ,,	124.40 ,,
100 kilometres ...	132.0 ,,	124.17 ,,
100 miles ...	135.1 ,,	119.01 ,,
200 kilometres ...	136.6 ,,	118.88 ,,
One hour	137.4 ,,	119.01 ,,
AMERICAN CLASS F :		
25 kilometres	132.6 ,,	none
25 miles ...	133.1 ,,	132.4 ,,
50 kilometres ...	133.4 ,,	none
50 miles ...	134.7 ,,	131.1 ,,
75 kilometres ...	134.5 ,,	none
75 miles ...	136.5 ,,	none
100 kilometres ...	135.8 ,,	none
100 miles ...	137.7 ,,	131.8 ,,
200 kilometres ...	139.1 ,,	none
One hour ...	139.3 ,,	66.04 ,,

During the short period of Lt. Col. Gardner's stay in Utah, a standard TD M.G., driven by Dick van Osten, captured a total of 23 American stock car Class F records, culminating in the 12-hour record at an average speed of 75.34 m.p.h. Altogether, a good week for M.G.s!

Celebration : Goldie Gardner (white helmet) is fifth from the right.

TWO THOUSAND MILES IN A TD M.G.

Some Editorial Impressions and Incidents During a Recent High-Speed Trip to Italy

THERE is nothing like a full week of high-speed motoring on the Continent to enable one to judge a car's capabilities. The recent Italian Grand Prix at Monza afforded us the opportunity to take over a perfectly standard TD M.G., which was used to transport two people and quite a considerable amount of baggage to the famous circuit and back.

It should be made clear that this was a normal Abingdon demonstrator, with absolutely nothing in the way of stage-two tuning, special axle ratio, high compression cylinder head or other non-standard equipment. It already had many thousands of hard miles on the clock, and during the period it was in our hands, apart from the usual POW and tyre pressure drills, no tinkering whatsoever was necessary. A continental touring box of spares was carried but never opened. As a matter of fact, the box was left by mistake in a Milan hotel, and the AA has undertaken to see it safely back to England again.

The excellent all-weather equipment on the TD was a blessing. On the way to Dover we ran into a cloudburst, which reduced speed to something under 20 m.p.h. and caused us to miss the Townsend Ferry by something under five minutes. Fortunately, Dunkirk was still having the lock gates trouble which delayed the B.R.M. expedition, and we were able to ship the M.G. on the train ferry, which was

being diverted to Calais. On arrival at Calais harbour the wretched currents made manœuvring difficult, and we sat outside the French port for five hours.

No sooner had the hood been lowered on the way out of Calais than the rains came—real push-rod stuff which tries the patience of even the hardiest of spartans. The other half of the crew suggested timidly that it would be less wet with a roof, to the great relief of the driver who erected the hood in record time.

A remarkable experience on the road to Arras was driving through legions of large frogs, which kept popping up and down in the headlights' glare. Anyway, it is quite something to be able to say that one has skidded on a carpet of squashed frogs—ugh!

We stopped overnight at Arras. The run down next day to Switzerland was wonderful. For kilometre after kilometre the little M.G. hummed along at a comfortable 5,000 r.p.m. (72 m.p.h.). At this cruising speed the power-unit is delightfully sweet, and fuel consumption is satisfyingly low, being around 25 m.p.g., which, with "supercarburant" at over five bob a gallon, is a point worth considering. Some people have criticized the 5.50 x 15 ins. tyres and the 5.125 to 1 axle ratio as being rather unfair to the power-plant. We must say that the car does not give the impression that it is being over-revved. The very willing push-rod engine

appears to revel in r.p.m. Admittedly it has quite a bit of weight to push around—the TD turns the scale at over 17 cwt. (dry)—and the classic Abingdon contours have little in the way of anti-drag properties. It comes as a pleasant surprise to discover that the Midget has such a brisk and effortless performance with a crew and luggage to transport as well.

Whilst on a critical note, there is no gainsaying the fact that the i.f.s. M.G. does have a certain amount of over-steering characteristic. However, after one becomes used to the car, this characteristic appears to become lessened to the extent of not being noticeable at all. In fact, it would go so far as to say that after a few hundred miles the general road-worthiness of the TD improves out of all recognition. Whether or not this is due to the driver rapidly acquiring "TD technique" is difficult to say, but the fact remains that there are few cars safer to drive under all possible types of road conditions than the M.G. Midget.

The car is a joy to handle in the Alps. We crossed the Simplon Pass in deplorable weather and with the roads as greasy as they could possibly be. Swirling mist added to the general discomfort, and we give full marks to this fine little car for conveying to the crew a complete sense of confidence in its ability to go strictly in the direction in which it is pointed.

An amusing interlude concerns a

Dutch coach, a Citroën towing a trailer on which was a motor launch, and one of those twisty Simplon tunnels. The Citroën driver let the M.G. pass at the first opportunity, but we soon overhauled the coach on top of which was a mountain of luggage. It was raining so heavily at this period, that the M.G. driver had wound a bright green towel round his head.

Contretemps

We followed the coach into the tunnel, but when trying to take the sharp right-hand bend inside, the vehicle jammed itself thoroughly on the low roof. Behind us came the Citroën. Reversing that unwieldly trailer safely out of the tunnel was a tribute to the skill of the French car's driver. Only by letting down the tyres, and removing the heap of luggage was it possible to free the coach, and in the midst of these operations, we heard in the distance the peculiar trumpet-horn of one of the Swiss postal cars.

A desperate race against time followed, for nothing must impede the progress of a Swiss postal vehicle. After dozens of attempts, the coach was finally backed out successfully. To our amazement, the Dutch passengers were helpless with laughter. Apparently the sight of the M.G., plastered from bonnet to tail with Alpine mud, and the driver looking like the Caliph of Baghdad, sitting cross-legged on the front bumper, was something not easily forgotten—particularly as the Citroën crew had unhitched the trailer, and were busy fiddling with their boat.

The complete anti-climax was the appearance of the Swiss "postal car", which turned out to be an American jeep fitted with a passable imitation of the exclusive trumpet-horns.

On the way down to Domodossola, we overtook a couple of Swiss-owned TDs, one of which was so festooned with gadgets that it was scarcely recognizable as a product of Abingdon. The spare wheel had a chromium-plated cover; there were two reversing lights, a plated luggage grid, and double bumper bars. A fishing-rod radio aerial was surmounted by a pennant. Aero screens, "Perspex" wind deflectors, anti-dazzle screens, and a couple of swivelling spot-lamps made the cockpit area look a trifle crowded. The front-end was even more bewildering. The badges of probably every motor club in Europe strove manfully to peep through no less than four pass-lights, and a pair of matched triple-trumpet horns. Anyway the white-helmeted occupants gave us a cheery wave, and the M.G. thumbs-up signal.

We stayed the night in Stresa on the shores of lovely Lake Maggiore. Next day we had the pleasure of being passed by a Ferrari coupé travelling at well over 100 m.p.h.—the Ferrari not the M.G.—on the autostrada to Milan. The TD romped along happily at 5,800 r.p.m. (just over 83 m.p.h.) for a couple of kilometres or so, just to show the driver of an Aurelia that British sports-cars can also do a spot of autostrada-burning.

Taking stock after arriving at Milan, we found that up till then the TD had averaged 26 m.p.g. since leaving England, and had used rather less than $1\frac{1}{2}$ pints of oil. On the Belfort to Besancon section we succeeded in putting exactly 61 miles into the hour on dry roads. From the entry to the autostrada at Seste-Callente, to the Milan outlet (about 22 miles), the car averaged 74 m.p.h. A deaf old woman near Vevey owed her life to the excellence of the Lockheed brakes.

A Real Traffic Test

Returning from Monza after the Italian G.P., we took part in a Grand Prix of our own which came to an abrupt halt at the bridge in the town. The traffic jam was far worse than the first Silverstone, and vehicles moved in fits and starts whilst dozens of Lambretta and Vespa scooters scuttled hazardously whenever a couple of square inches of roadway appeared. It was like that all the way to Milan, and the TD was seldom in a higher gear than second.

Next day we set off for home. Once again the M.G. had her head on the autostrada with a joyous note from an engine made contented by really decent fuel. The difference between Continental "super" and Britain's power-paralyzing Pool is extraordinary: no pinking, no running-on and a grand feeling of having bags of power in hand.

This time we had no Simplon adventures, and the run settled down to putting as many kilometres into the hour as and when road conditions permitted. On the Italian-Swiss frontier, near Domodossola, we met up with a London taxi, loaded to the limit with baggage and four hefty occupants. It did not possess a hackney plate, so it must have been one of those £50 bargains one sees advertized. Anyway, it was plodding steadily up the mountain roads.

The M.G. was passed by only one car during the entire distance from Milan to Calais—and that was by Raymond Mays in a Ford Zephyr.

Taking it by and large, the TD M.G. appears to be an ideal car for Continental road work. It is fairly economical, extremely lively and capable of putting up excellent average speeds. Its performance in the Alps is almost an eye-opener, and explains the reason why the M.G. is such a firm favourite with the Swiss. Incidentally, one Swiss owner remarked on the absence of oil and water temperature gauges, and suggested that these instruments are very desirable fitments in Alpine territory.

A detailed account of actual performance figures obtained on test will appear in a forthcoming article on the TD.

G.

Familiar sight to pre-war enthusiasts; the entrance to Wetherby Grange, where the Yorkshire Sports Car Club used to hold their speed trials.

Just Over the Border

A BRISK RUN TO SCOTLAND BY TD M.G.

IT so happened a short time ago that I was faced with the prospect of making my second long run up the Great North Road within the space of a fortnight, this time to attend the very successful race meeting run on the airfield circuit at Winfield by the Berwick, Lothian and Hawick and District clubs. (Those names always make me feel that there should be a snappy little couplet about them, on the lines of the waiter. the porter and the upstairs maid—but I can never quite get it.) Anyway, there was this journey. Of course, I could have done what many probably much saner people did, and gone by the night train to Berwick-upon-Tweed, but, after all, I don't work for the Railway Travellers' Journal, and the car run is always more interesting.

So I decided to go by car; but in order to avoid doing the same run twice in such a short space of time in the same car I went to ask the Editor if he had any idea where there was a nice fast car which I could borrow for the trip. He said no, which didn't surprise me; but what did surprise me was the fact that later on in the same day he summoned me once more, to tell me that after all he had managed to do something for me in this matter (adding the usual rider about not knowing why on earth he should go to so much trouble on my behalf, but there it was) and that P. M. Walters, a director of Jarvis of Wimbledon, had offered a trial of his TD M.G. two-seater, which would be just the car for the job.

Now this is no ordinary TD, as it has been modified to stage 2 of the M.G. tuning manual; that is to say, the compression ratio has been raised to 9.3 to 1, the ports have been enlarged and oversize valves fitted. In addition, this particular car had higher-than-standard back axle gearing of 4.55 to 1 (for competition purposes this would probably prove a shade too high, but for fast touring it resulted in a pleasantly high cruising speed without the feeling of over-stressing the engine). So it was with a feeling of pleasurable anticipation that I collected the car from Jarvis' one recent Friday afternoon.

Late Start

As the first of the Show Numbers of *The Autocar* was already out, and the second was casting its heavy shadow over the editorial offices, it proved impossible to leave London as soon as I had hoped. In fact, it was rapidly approaching eight o'clock in the evening before I finally managed to struggle clear of the official establishment; and as the actual racing was due to start at 2 p.m. the following day, and I had no intention of foregoing my beauty sleep, it was obvious that some fairly serious motoring would be necessary. Fortunately, I had co-opted for the arduous position of navigator one Pat Stephenson, an old friend of mine (well, not so old—but you know what I mean), who had filled that difficult spot on many occasions in the past, right from the days when together we founded the original *Scuderia Impecuniosa*, more years ago than I care to remember. So I was at least certain that there would be no complaints from that quarter.

Well, we attired ourselves in suitable Arctic-style clothing, as most of the pleasure of a run in an open car disappears if you are forced to have the hood up, and set off over Blackfriars Bridge and through the purlieus of North London by my own peculiar and devious traffic-avoiding route. Long before we had left the Metropolis behind it was obvious to us both that this was no ordinary Midget; its acceleration in the lower gears was vivid, and the special supplementary hand ignition control proved valuable in controlling the tendency to detonate, which was noticeable in spite of a liberal proportion of Octol in the fuel.

A gruesome twosome at journey's end!

Then we had left speed limits behind, and were purring up the familiar route to the north on a beautiful crisp autumn evening. At Grantham we decided to try to make Bawtry before stopping for the night; so a swift telephonic wrestle was indulged in, as a result of which the hospitable Crown Hotel in that township agreed to await our arrival, which eventually took place at roughly 11.30 p.m. And so, gratefully, to bed.

Saturday morning dawned—and with it the realization that a considerable area of the north of England was buried beneath an opaque blanket of fog. Consequently, it was nine o'clock or more before the M.G. once more took the road to Scotland, and for the first 30 miles or so progress was by no means meteoric. During this period driver and navigator agreed that the whole idea of going up for the week-end by car was just plain stupid anyway, that we were getting too old for this sort of thing, that we were already too old for this sort of car (although at least you could see out of it in foggy weather), and so forth; but then the sun came through the mist and things improved considerably.

The M.G.'s high compression ratio necessitated the addition of a proportion of Octol at each refuelling stop.

Behind Schedule

It was then that the potentialities of the car really became apparent, for we were well behind schedule. Mile after mile was covered at an easy cruising speed of an indicated 4,800-5,000 r.p.m. (which, allowing for a degree of instrumental optimism and other imponderables, represents something in the region of 80 m.p.h.), and in spite of threading our way through the whole length of Newcastle-upon-Tyne and its satellites, not to mention the traffic on its way to Winfield, we arrived in Berwick at 1 p.m., and at the circuit twenty minutes later. And the meeting itself was well worth the trouble, providing a good variety of races and including many keenly fought battles.

It is a pity that many of the Scottish drivers come down south but rarely, so that the majority of the spectators who go to Silverstone and Goodwood, for instance, never see them in action. Ninian Sanderson, Ian Sutherland, Alex McGlashan are three of the names in the half-litre brigade which readily spring to mind, while the ingenious specials of Ian Hopper and Jim Gibbon are two cars which would not disgrace themselves in comparable company anywhere in these islands. Of these two, incidentally, the former employs a Lea-Francis engine in a J.P. chassis, with a two-seater sports body, and is rumoured to be the prototype of a line of J.P. sports cars, while the latter ran in trials

As straight as the eye can see: the New Bedford River, which cuts across the fens from Earith to Downham Market. It was dug to provide drainage for the low-lying countryside.

These beautiful almshouses will strike a chord in the memory of most users of the Great North Road.

JUST OVER THE BORDER . . . . *continued*

The six-bladed prop is no modern invention

and speed trials last year as the Girastro Rover, and represents much hard work and practical development.

The spectators—who turned up in very large numbers—loved every minute of it, while the autograph hunters were as active as at any race meeting anywhere. When all the tumult and the shouting had died down, Pat and I turned the nose of the Midget southward again, recrossed the Border, and eventually reached Darlington before night had fallen too heavily, and there stayed for the night.

Fine and Dry

The following morning—Sunday—although not too promising as far as the weather was concerned, was at least fine and dry. Off we went again, down the Great North Road; but although we had hoped for a reasonably clear run on this section of the trip, we found that there were almost as many heavy lorries about as on week-days. Among the various peculiar loads we noticed in course of transportation, pride of place must go to an enormous drying tower; here the navigator insisted on my hovering in the overtaking position for what seemed like several minutes while he took a photograph of the device. We also got involved in a discussion on steering characteristics, as a result of which we went twice round one roundabout while I proved that the M.G. did, in fact, possess a slight tendency to oversteer.

After Newark we left the direct route and branched off to Sleaford, as we were making for the Newmarket side of Cambridge, where the navigator lives. This involved a long journey over the Fen country, which never fails to stir within me memories of summer holidays in my youth, always spent in Norfolk; down to Holbeach, across to Long Sutton, thence to Wisbech, Littleport and Ely; across many of the famous drains such as the Forty-Foot Drain and the New Bedford River, laid down years ago as part of the

eternal fight against the flooding of this low-lying territory. Ely was alive with people and cars, flocking towards its famous cathedral for the annual Harvest Festival service; and then in no time we were at our destination, and the navigator disembarked. Later I restarted for the solo run back to London, always a fast journey by night down A11, then to Royston and Baldock, then a bit of the Great North Road again, and finally the Barnet by-pass.

So the week-end finished; throughout the 740 miles covered the M.G. never gave a sign of trouble, and behaved perfectly. In all fairness to the car it should be said that really, for a compression ratio as high as that employed in this instance, petrol-benzole is a necessity if the best is to be got out of the engine; but in spite of the absence of that valuable commodity, the performance was quite remarkable on a mixture of Pool and Octol. There were, of course, certain points about the car which I criticized; but I have never yet met the car which was beyond reproach in every way. The handling is good, being a great advance on previous models by virtue of the use of i.f.s. of relative softness, while the power extracted nowadays from the familiar Midget engine gets more and more surprising. In every respect this trip was a great success.

J. A. C.

Navigator and steed pose beneath the familiar sign : Scotland won't be long now!

ANOTHER LEASE OF LIFE FOR SILVERSTONE

THE future of Silverstone has at last been settled, as a motor racing circuit; it is now announced that the circuit will be taken over by the B.R.D.C. on January 1, 1952, for a period of four years (national emergencies, and so on, permitting). The B.R.D.C. will operate it on the same sort of basis as the R.A.C. have done; in other words, it will continue to be available for the use of other motor clubs.

This is a piece of good news, and most of the credit for this state of affairs must go to Desmond Scannell, the energetic secretary of the B.R.D.C. While Silverstone is certainly not ideal as a circuit, yet until we have something much better we cannot

afford to lose it, and the number of racing miles covered there in the last year or two must be very considerable indeed. Besides the club meetings held there at an average of twelve a year, it has been the circuit for many major meetings, amongst them the Grand Prix of Europe in 1950, and has drawn such crowds as to cause a considerable traffic problem on the roads by which it is approached, though in this last season special traffic schemes by the police of the counties concerned did much to improve the situation. The first important event at Silverstone in the 1952 programme is to be the fourth International *Daily Express* meeting on May 10.

AUG. 1951,
BONNEVILLE SALT FLATS, UTAH

STANDARD MG TD SETS
23 AMERICAN STOCK CAR RECORDS
AT 75.34 M.P.H.
FOR 12 HOURS!

A stock MG TD taken under the supervision of the AAA, from a dealer's showroom in Salt Lake City, established 23 new American Class F stock car records by completing a 12-hour run at an average speed of **75.34** miles per hour, thereby creating records for all distances from 25 kilometers to 1000 kilometers. Another proof of the MG's reliability and speed.

(All records made under supervision of the American Automobile Association and subject to confirmation.)

AMERICA'S MOST POPULAR SPORTS CAR

HAMBRO TRADING COMPANY OF AMERICA, INC.
SOLE CONCESSIONAIRES FOR MG—MORRIS—RILEY
350 FIFTH AVENUE, NEW YORK 1, NEW YORK

Lester-M.G.

The low build and businesslike appearance of the car are well shown in this three-quarter front view, with Harry Lester, the designer and constructor, at the wheel.

SUCCESSFUL SPORTS-RACING CAR NOW IN LIMITED PRODUCTION

DURING the last two seasons the name Lester-M.G. has appeared more and more frequently in race reports and results, usually with additional comment as to the surprising speed developed by this attractive and workmanlike little car. This, however, is not really surprising to those who know Harry Lester, for this enthusiast has worked on M.G. cars for a good many years, and has produced a succession of special versions thereof, each faster than the last.

The present model first appeared in prototype form in one or two minor sprint events during the summer of 1949. Since then it has been steadily improved, until finally the decision was taken to produce it in limited quantities; in all nearly a dozen examples have now been constructed, and several of these have distinguished themselves in races and speed events in the hands of Harry Lester himself, J. C. C. Mayers and P. W. Griffith. Several cars have also been exported to the U.S.A.; and in view of the demand from that quarter, and the fact that the production is arbitrarily limited to some twelve cars per annum by component supplies, for the present at least this market must take precedence, leaving—as usual—nothing for the poor home motorist.

The basis of the car is a plain and straightforward tubular chassis frame, of Lester design and construction; this consists in the main of two 3in diameter 16 s.w.g., 45-ton tensile strength steel tubular side members, with two cross members of the same material and a third of smaller diameter. At the front the standard M.G. pressed steel cross member is used. The front suspension utilizes M.G. wishbones and swivel pins, but the coil springs are special (as the car is much lighter than the standard M.G.) and Woodhead-Monroe telescopic dampers are fitted.

The steering gear is again entirely new; instead of the M.G. rack and pinion assembly, a Bishop cam-type steering box (made specially for the cars, and incorporating a light-alloy casing) is mounted on outrigger brackets from the front cross member on the right side, and a similar bracket on the left carries the pivot for a slave arm; a three-piece track rod connects up the assembly. The rear suspension is by special Woodhead leaf springs, sliding in traditional M.G. fashion in trunnions at the rear end and damped by telescopic Woodhead-Monroe units. The rear axle is actually a TC M.G. assembly, slightly modified at the ends to take the different hubs and wheels used in this application.

The engine is basically the TD M.G. unit, but the block is bored out 3mm, making the bore 72mm and the cubic capacity 1,462 c.c. The engine is brought up to Stage 2 of the M.G. tuning process; that is to say, the compression ratio is raised to 9.2 to 1, the inlet ports are bored out and larger inlet valves fitted. In this form, running on 80-octane fuel (which suits the engine perfectly), it is estimated that between 80 and 85 b.h.p. are developed at approximately 6,200 r.p.m. Two S.U. carburettors are used, and the

SPECIFICATION

Engine.—M.G., four cylinders 72 × 90 mm (1,462 c.c.), o.h.v., push-rod. Compression ratio 9.2 to 1. Two S.U. carburettors, coil ignition. Approx. 80 b.h.p. at 6,200 r.p.m.

Transmission.—M.G. TC gear box and rear axle; overall ratios 4.875, 6.59, 9.51 and 16.48 to 1.

Suspension.—Independent front by wishbones and coil springs; half-elliptic rear. Woodhead-Monroe telescopic dampers front and rear.

Brakes.—Lockheed hydraulic, 9in diameter by 1½in wide, working in Al-fin drums. Central fly-off hand brake operating by cable on rear wheels only.

Fuel System.—S.U. electric pump, 12-gallon rear tank.

Tyres and Wheels.—5.00-16in Michelin tyres on bolt-on steel wheels.

Main Dimensions.—Wheelbase 7ft 8in, track (front) 4ft 0½in, (rear) 3ft 11in. Dry weight 10½cwt, distributed in the following proportions: 55 per cent on front wheels, 45 per cent on rear.

Manufacturers.—H. Lester (Cars), Ltd., Bath Road, Thatcham, Berkshire.

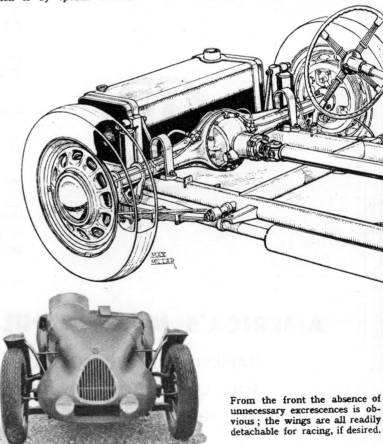

From the front the absence of unnecessary excrescences is obvious; the wings are all readily detachable for racing, if desired.

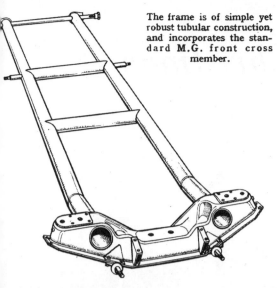

The frame is of simple yet robust tubular construction, and incorporates the standard M.G. front cross member.

Cockpit view, showing the plain and practical layout of controls and instruments.

manifolding throughout is Lester's own, fabricated as a welded unit.

The gear box is a standard TC M.G. unit, chosen because it is rather shorter and also some 10lb lighter than the later pattern. A normal Hardy-Spicer propeller-shaft completes the transmission line; at present the TC axle ratio, of 4.875 to 1, is fitted, but plans are afoot for the production of "higher" ratios (that is, with lower indices). The brakes are Lockheed hydraulic, of the type used in the 1¼-litre M.G. saloon, working in this instance in Al-Fin drums. The pressed steel perforated wheels are of Morris Ten type, carrying 5.50 by 16in Michelin tyres.

On this chassis is mounted a simple and good-looking two-seater body, panelled in 18 s.w.g. aluminium alloy. No doors are provided, but the steering wheel is quickly detachable to give ease of ingress for the driver; an upswept cowl surmounted by a Perspex shield deflects the wind, and a fold-flat aero screen is mounted in front of the passenger, the obligatory second mirror for racing purposes being mounted on this in the folded position. A 12-gallon fuel tank shares the tail of the body with the spare wheel; both this tank and the radiator are of Gallay manufacture. Fuel feed is by S.U. electric pump. The simple panel layout incorporates rev counter, speedometer, oil pressure gauge, and oil and water thermometers. At present, incidentally, a cooling duct is fitted to direct air round the sump, but plans include a larger sump and an oil radiator.

A brief trial of the car in rather damp and unfavourable circumstances proved it to possess road-holding and steering qualities of an extremely high order; it would not be too high praise to say that the handling of the machine is quite exceptional for a light car, and far better than that of many classic and larger cars. The light weight—only 10½ cwt dry—coupled with the high output, gives terrific acceleration, and 6,000 r.p.m. on top gear was easily reached, representing approximately 95 m.p.h.; this could unquestionably have been exceeded had road conditions permitted.

The Lester-M.G., in short, represents a very workmanlike and sensibly constructed small super-sports car, in a class which possesses all too few representatives from this country. It will be coveted by many, and the only trouble is that it can be possessed only by the very few.   J. A. C.

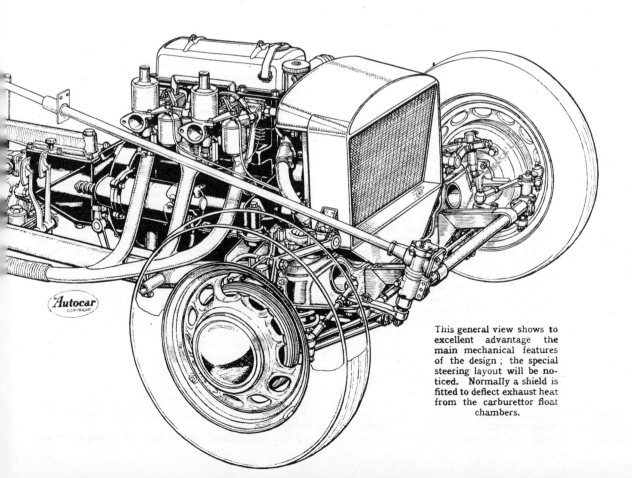

This general view shows to excellent advantage the main mechanical features of the design; the special steering layout will be noticed. Normally a shield is fitted to deflect exhaust heat from the carburettor float chambers.

Sports Car for Christmas

THE man who receives a present at Christmas, or on his birthday, often shouts, "It's just what I wanted." Whether or not this is wholly sincere is another matter, but the exigencies of Aunt Matilda are stern. Happy the man who can shout it with conviction. The car that provided my transport last Christmas was very much what I wanted, and it may be suitable to recall it before the recollections of the season of seasons have wholly disappeared in the austere resolutions symbolized so well by January, when motoring itself becomes much less comfortable. A journey home at Christmas is always good, and when it is in an appropriate car then it approaches the sublime. This period afterwards is one that I always feel the old Christmas poem described so well.

> After Crystenmasse, comes the crabbed Lenten,
> Frighting our flesh.

If I had been asked, as the season approached, what would be my choice of a vehicle for this hypothetical journey to South Devon I would have suggested a car somewhat rugged—to agree with the season—nothing saloony or summery, a car representative of that bracing physical atmosphere that surrounds us in December. One of the memories that must lie very deep in the collective unconscious of Christmas is the Gothic juxtaposition of cold without and warmth within. As I thought about this not impossible car it began already to seem more real than, say, a car on a Christmas card. My notion of a route to Devon had already formed, and I began to see, against a *décor* provided by the Berkshire Downs, a green-lit instrument panel. For once it did not matter if the instruments were a little hard to read when travelling at speed, but they had to be mounted beneath swept scuttles. My hypothetical bonnet had to *be* a bonnet, and not the nose of a jet aeroplane, and the wings must be clearly defined. A car, in fact, in keeping with the traditional nature of Christmas. If it made me a little stiff, and a little chilly, then I would be all the better pleased.

First-stage Tuning

How curious then (and who said that the red-jacketed fellow with a predilection for chimneys does not exist?) that an M.G., TD version, should turn up about December 23. And no ordinary TD at that, for it had a much increased compression ratio and larger valves; it was in that first stage of the process, by means of facilities available from the company, which eventually converts it from a sturdy and moderately fast sports car to one that will travel in excess of 85 m.p.h. There were my engine, and the square-cut bonnet that enclosed it, just as I had imagined them.

A previous driver and colleague, with the generosity of a Father Christmas, had left a few gallons of benzole in the tank, and this octane-for-Christmas was a gesture I appreciated. When compression ratios get much above seven—and this modified car has a ratio of about eight to one—then that hater of the festive season, Jacob Marley, with his clanking chain made up of cashboxes and detonation, seems to get inside the head of most cars. As the benzole became diluted with worse fuel on the journey, I had to console myself with thinking that perhaps the undeveloped races of the world, in Persia and elsewhere, were receiving the benefit of the better fuel. At any rate I hoped so, but not without a slight and (even at this season) irritating thought that the reactionary bureaucratic habits of mind of some ministry might be responsible. It may be that just as a former Under-Secretary to a ministry said that the human inside is equally satisfied with Stilton and Australian cheddar, the engine of a car cannot tell the difference

The Christmas seat, with all conveniences, including a defroster, and the hood available in case of need.

between . . . but no more need be said on the lugubrious subject.

All London seemed to have escaped for Christmas long before the afternoon of the Eve, and the Great West Road had that deserted air that shivered one's spine in the film *Seven Days to Noon.* I reflected, with this in mind, that even supposing some mad idealist did blow up the Metropolis before my return, I would not greatly care. Even the traffic lights shone like crême-de-menthe and holly berries, through Slough and Maidenhead, and along the strange neon-world that extends past Heathrow and along A4. My route was intended to avoid A30, the more usual route to the West.

The alternative, for those interested, is a little longer, but provides good motoring. It follows A4 through Hungerford and Marlborough as far as Beckhampton, then takes A361 for a short dash across the downs to Devizes, after which A350 is intersected and followed through Warminster to intersect finally with A303; this excellent and interesting road leads into Devon and meets the notorious A30 itself. Designing alternatives to A30 could almost become a parlour game.

A halt at Devizes for fuel—no benzole, so the clanking cashboxes must be endured. It had begun to rain by then. The old-fashioned Christmas weather was hardly to be expected, but when well into Wiltshire an immense wuthering of rain and wind contributed to the hoped-for Gothic atmosphere. The head lamps, which might actually be a little more powerful on this tuned-up car, left one floating in an illuminated globe of rain and wind. Wind that was strong enough to pluck the nose of the TD sideways when at speed. Those moments, worst for driving, which are neither dark nor light, were, on Christmas Eve, enchanting, with tiny lights appearing yellowly here and there among the folds of the downs, tanned by the winter.

I never realized before how clever the Wessex peasant is at camouflage. With a liberal covering of his native soil, an old Home Guard jacket, and corduroy, he is pretty well unsnipable. When in the middle of the road at dimmity, on the other hand, he is equally invisible, but much more vulnerable. Fortunately, all those that I met reached their hearthsides safely.

The driver was dressed for the part. A friend muttered

The knots derive in part from twin S.U. carburettors, in this instance with twin fuel pumps.

The Christmas spirit is a strong solvent. Why exactly a familiar route should seem different at this time is not plain. A bouquet to Warminster, for its fine illuminated Christmas tree standing in the churchyard; there was an atmosphere of frantic but contented shopping in all towns. Even the café where I stopped for a quick cup of tea was irrationally Christmassy, and highly unbusinesslike, with early parties beginning behind half-open parlour doors, and the thump and shriek of raucous but seasonable children. Curtain corners showed coloured chains of decorations.

The feel of sports car motoring, which seemed so right at this time, is made up of a certain lowness and hardness—this is still true of the M.G. although it has a now conventional front suspension. Firmness means that there is always a horizon of bonnet, and this car was virtually without roll. One is more " in " the car, and nearer the road, and there is a sense of belonging to it which is entirely lacking in the comforts of the enormous bench seat motoring of modern saloons. Controls, too, are comfortably at the ready, with the short stiff gear lever and, best of all, the fly-off hand brake. Fresh air, too, in reasonable quantities is welcome even in these air-conditioned times. The engine of the TD is not afraid of revolutions. In this initial stage of tuning there is a useful increase of power.

In bad weather, at night, it is nice amusement to judge the point of cut-off on bends from the curvature of the cats' eyes, as they lead away in front, and Wiltshire and Devon provided plenty of this. There is a deceptive straightness on some stretches which will suddenly wind into a bend which increases its curve with compound interest. By the time Honiton was reached the demister had proved its value, and traffic in front was sloshing up an obfuscating cloud of brown spray. There was no need to stay behind for long, for the M.G., by reason of its immense handiness, can soon put its nose in front.

There was not a lot of traffic to pass, and much of the pleasure of this run came from the feeling of dashing through a sombre landscape, deserted, as if the last inhabitant of the globe was racing to keep the final Christmas of all. Holiday times always provide the unexpected in traffic conditions. The destination, a South Devon resort of the more fashionable kind, shows at this season an almost Wenceslas-like generosity in providing a great deal of illumination for a moderate number of deserving visitors. Approaching it from the higher ground that slopes off Dartmoor—to pursue the image a little further—it was lit with the cosy twinkling warmth of a Christmas tree, against Torbay; there was a copy of the *Everest Supplement* of *The Times* by the fireside when I arrived, just to emphasize the point that the rugged way of doing things has a pleasure of its own.

J. F. H.

once, on seeing him in this guise, " *cucullus non fecit . . .*" which might be loosely Englished as " the duffel coat does not make the dicer " and however one may agree about the affectations of such coats in Chelsea, there is no doubt that in an open car on a long journey such a garment is useful. The large pockets are just right for holding loose cigarettes, an electric torch and the mutton cloth for wiping the screen. My predecessor of *The Autocar* Road Test team had arranged for the fitting of a Berkshire defroster, which showed prescience (not only in the name), as in appalling weather the square of vision was clear all the time.

Traditional weather was a month behind the author. A photograph taken last week on the route as it crosses Salisbury Plain.

the unit to overheat; in point of fact, under normal road conditions the engine is, if anything, rather over-cooled.

Practically no modifications were required to the Cooper chassis, beyond the fitting of Mintex racing brake linings to the 2LS Lockheed system, and the employment of an ENV 4 to 1 rear axle. A 24-gallon fuel tank is housed in the tail, whilst a rear locker contains the spare wheel and provides a surprising amount of space for carrying odds and ends. As an added safety precaution, Cliff Davis has cleverly contrived padded knee rests in the

The 1½-LITRE COOPER-M.G.

Test Impressions of the 114 m.p.h. Two-seater Which Caused Such a Sensation at the Opening Goodwood Meeting

OUT of Abingdon, by Surbiton, influenced by Modena, realized by Leonard and developed by Davis—that, in a nutshell, describes what is assuredly the fastest and most delightful, unsupercharged sports-car in Great Britain at the present time. Why this country does not reproduce this type of machine in mild quantity for the export market is something of a mystery. Here we have a light-weight vehicle of infinite charm, which, by its performance at the opening Goodwood meeting on 22nd March, proved beyond argument that it is more than a match for any car in its class.

Originally conceived by Lionel Leonard, the "Cooperari" is basically one of the standard Cooper sports chassis. Body work is un-ashamedly Ferrari Mille Miglia, with decidedly more handsome contours due to a lower build and altogether slimmer outline. The power-unit is TC/TD M.G. bored out to give almost 1,500 c.c., and fitted with a Stage 2 type of cylinder head incorporating several Leonard mods., KE 965 valves, Martlet pistons, large-bore S.U. carburetters and other aids to ultimate performance. The Leonard-Davis engine was the direct outcome of the extremely

successful 1,250 c.c. TC unit assembled by George Phillips for his 1949/50 Le Mans two-seater. Indeed, the Cooper-M.G. had one of Phillips's engines installed in it last year.

Careful tuning and meticulous assembly has resulted in a 1½-litre, push-rod engine, developing approximately 85 b.h.p. at 5,800 r.p.m., with an 8 to 1 compression ratio, and running on Esso 80 octane fuel. It will run well over 6,000 r.p.m. without a suspicion of detonation or any sign of valve-bounce. Indeed, for a four-cylinder unit of such proved potency the M.G. possesses exceptional smoothness, allied to almost perfect traffic manners. No fan is fitted, but it is impossible to cause

driving compartment to prevent any tendency for the driver to slide about on the seat during a race.

Cliff generously offered his car to AUTOSPORT for the week-end before the Goodwood meeting, an offer which was accepted with alacrity. Several hundreds of miles were covered within the space of a couple of days, including acceleration and maximum speed tests, and finishing up with some fast circuits of Goodwood on members' practice day. During the period the car was in our hands it behaved impeccably. The engine never lost the sharp edge of its tune, and one was left with the impression that it would run for ever at near maximum r.p.m.

The neat tail contains a fairly commodious locker, carrying spare wheel, tools and so on.

With only the driver in the car, the handling of the Cooper-M.G. is beyond criticism. However, with a crew whose weight totals some 26 stone, there is evidence of slight oversteer characteristics, which may, or may not, be due to over-suppleness of the transverse leaf springs. At first, the brakes were disappointing and appeared to require more pedal pressure than one is normally accustomed to with hydraulics. After about 100 miles of fast road-work, the linings bedded down rapidly, and the system improved almost beyond belief. We learned that brand-new linings had just been fitted, ready for the opening of the racing season.

With two up, there was a slight suspicion that the clutch was not quite up to the power-output of the 1½-litre engine, as a certain amount of slip was experienced during rapid take-off from standstill. As this is the standard TD M.G. unit, it was obviously not designed to transmit over 80 b.h.p. Nevertheless, with only the driver at the wheel, there is no trace of slip whatsoever. Wheel-spin is strangely absent on the car, giving proof of good engine torque and excellent weight distribution. The road adhesion during rapid acceleration has to be tried to be

speed figures, and are also able to give the approximate maximum speeds in the gears as recorded on the revolution-counter, and worked out according to the Dunlop formula. The maximum will surprise all sports-car owners. Over a measured distance, and taking an average of four runs (two in each direction), the Cooper-M.G. recorded 112.8 m.p.h. The fastest run (slight following wind) worked out at 114.6 m.p.h.—with the r.p.m. indicator needle well past the "six thou" mark crossing the line.

These figures will help to appreci-

★

(*Right*) *The M.G. engine is set well back in the frame; the bonnet lid is secured by quick-release screws.*

(*Below*) . . . *handling of the Cooper-M.G. is beyond criticism. It is seen here during some fast cornering on an East Anglian airfield circuit.*

★

eight gallons of fuel in the tank, oil, water, spare wheel, battery, lamps, dynamo, starter, etc., the Cooper-M.G. scales just 11 cwt. 2 lb. This gives a starting line p.w.r. of over 150 b.h.p. per ton, which is roughly similar to a good J.A.P.-engined Cooper "500".

As we said at the beginning of this article, the type of car which is exemplified by the admirable Leonard-Davis machine would make a valuable contribution to our high-performance car exports in the highly specialized market for sports-racing cars. It is delightfully simple

appreciated, and this undoubtedly contributes largely to the exceptional acceleration possessed by the car. Under very favourable weather conditions, with practically no wind, and on a dry concrete surface, a standing quarter-mile was accomplished in 18.25 secs., using all the gears. As no opportunity was available for checking the speedometer, it was decided to leave over figures which depend on the accuracy of the instrument until such times as it can be checked.

However we did obtain maximum

ate how Cliff Davis was able to lap the revised Goodwood circuit, which now includes a chicane, in a fraction under 1 min. 54 secs. (75.79 m.p.h.). The present sports-car record for the circuit stands to the credit of Oscar Moore and his XK 120 Jaguar-powered H.W.M. with 1 min. 53.2 secs. (76.73 m.p.h.)—3½ litres against 1½ litres.

The contributing factor to the remarkable performance of Cliff Davis's pretty little car is the excellent power-weight ratio. In full sports-car racing trim, with about

in general conception and is just the kind of machine which would make an instant appeal to the type of owner who prefers a highly individual vehicle.   G.

SPECIFICATION AND PERFORMANCE DATA

Engine: Four cylinders, o.h.v. (push-rod) M.G. 72 mm. x 90 mm. (1,467 c.c.), 85 b.h.p. at 5,800 r.p.m. with 8.3 to 1 c.r. and on Esso 80 Octane. Twin S.U. carburetters; sing'e S.U. fuel pump. Lucas coil and distributor.

Transmission: M.G. 4-speed gearbox; ratios, 4, 5.54, 8.28 and 14 to 1. Borg and Beck clutch; Hardy Spicer open propeller shaft; ENV spiral-bevel rear axle.

Suspension: Independent to all wheels by transverse leaf springs and wishbones; Girling hydraulic telescopic dampers.

General: Lucas 12-volt electrical equipment; rack and pinion steering; 24-gallon rear fuel tank; Cooper integral-brake-drum alloy wheels; 15 x 500 Dunlop tyres; Lockheed 2LS hydraulic brakes with Mintex linings. Wheelbase, 7 ft. 1 in. Track, 4 ft. 1 in. Ground clearance, 5½ ins. Weight (Wet, as tested), 11 cwt. 2 lbs.

Performance: Maximum speeds in gears: 1st, 33 m.p.h.; 2nd, 55 m.p.h.; 3rd, 83 m.p.h.; 4th, 114.6 m.p.h. Mean maximum (average 4 runs, 2 in each direction), 112.8 m.p.h. Standing ¼-mile, 18.25 secs. Average, 4 runs, 2 in each direction, 19.8 secs.

Chassis Manufacturers: The Cooper Car Co. Ltd., Ewell Road, Surbiton, Surrey.

The Stork a

the Sports Car

By Clayton E. Shaw, Jr.

IN THE HISTORIC valley of the Little Hoosick River and on the rugged mountain ranges that hem in the valley both to the east and west, the traditional stork is taking a terrific beating. His tongue hangs out and his tail droops as he attempts to outdistance John W. Little, country doctor, who resides with his family in the small village of Petersburg, N.Y. at the junction of New York routes 22 and 2.

The stork vs. doctor race has been held in this particular part of the country since the early 1700's, when the first settlers, trekking up from Connecticut and Rhode Island, found the only way into this beautiful valley to be over a well used Indian trail, complete with Indians.

These were tough days for the few itinerant doctors who traveled the rugged terrain on foot and horseback. For the stork, though, it was duck soup. He was usually the first one there.

With the coming of rough but passable roads, the "horse and buggy" doctor made things a little more difficult for the stork. The doc was beginning to hold his own in

stork and sports car

the age-long contest.

Today we are familiar with the modern country doctor pulling up to the farm house in his Detroit delivery wagon. His transportation is comfortable and dependable. He gives the stork an all-out race. The poor old stork has to live on a diet of high octane gas and really bore a hole through the air to get the checkered flag. He is a tough old bird and hard to discourage, but he is rapidly losing face as a result of numerous encounters with Doc Little.

An emergency phone call at Doc's house usually means a quick trip up winding mountain roads, brutal hold-overs from colonial days that do not appear on regular road maps. Before Doc Little became familiar with the rugged plateau country to the west, a topographical survey map of the area was his only guide.

In answer to an emergency call this young and personable doctor grabs his hat and bag in the manner of hundreds of other country doctors and rushes out to his garage. But from there on until he arrives at his destination all resemblance to the traditional rural physician ceases.

If you happened to be passing by at this particular time you would hear the sudden roar of a warming engine, and looking towards the open garage doors you'd get a fleeting glimpse of one of the neatest looking MG-TD's you ever laid eyes on. This is a sports car with a purpose; an MG that is proud and can hardly wait to dig its tire treads into the steep country roads to bring the doctor swiftly and safely to those so anxiously awaiting his arrival.

Several years ago someone gave Doc Little a ride in a sports car and a chance to drive it. That experience did what it is doing to thousands of people throughout the country—it kindled the burning desire to own and drive a sports car. So in May of 1951 he took the plunge and bought an MG.

Since that time this sturdy English thoroughbred has carried the Doc over thousands of miles of real pleasure driving while he makes his daily calls. This is a combination of business and pleasure in its truest sense: the pleasure of driving a sensitive, beautifully running and handling car, which in no way interferes with the serious business of being a doctor.

To keep the record straight it must be stated at this point that the Doc does not aspire to be a race driver. He will never enter and drive his car in a road race or hillclimb. There is no objection to these events from the Doc's point of view, he thinks they are great. However, he has a fine family and a demanding profession that leaves little time for anything else. Anyway, there is slight incentive for the Doc to envy the city dweller who drives his sports car several hundred miles to compete in a hillclimb. The Doc battles the mountains daily in his MG and thor-

oughly enjoys it. He is a practical sports car man.

Here in the practical use of a sports car is the great significance of Dr. Little and his MG. He represents that relatively small, but steadily increasing group of modern automobile pioneers who are breaking away from the conventional means of transportation and are adopting the use of some type of sports car for pleasurable daily travel.

For a young man to buy and drive a sports car in a sports car-minded community, surrounded by fellow car club members, is one thing. For a business or professional family man to appear driving such a chariot in a small rural town, where sports cars are practically unknown, is definitely something else. This hardy soul must be prepared with an agile sense of humor to parry the wise cracks, sly smiles, and even sneers, that come his way. This man is an automotive pioneer just as surely as was his compatriot who, in the early part of the century, was forced to bite his lip as he listened to the old cry, "Get a horse."

When the Doctor first appeared in his new sports job he encountered a certain amount of homespun humor directed at "that little thing" or "Dr. Little's little car." However, he soon found out, in every case, this was the result of a lack of understanding. A few well chosen demonstrations and explanations of the car's history and performance, plus the Doctor's enthusiastic willingness to answer any and all questions, wrought a quick and amazing change in the area.

Now "Doc Little's little car" is a respected member of the community. It makes its way over hill and dale, and parks beside its Detroit cousins without causing a stir or provoking comment. It has been "accepted." The Doc need make no more explanations. The car receives no more ridicule. It has become a solid and respected citizen, just like its owner.

It would be ideal to end this glimpse of the country doctor and his sports car with the thought that Doc Little lived happily ever after behind the wheel of his MG. Unfortunately this, indeed, would be a fairy tale. For in the true spirit of the pioneer and sports car enthusiast, Dr. Little is growing restless. His experiment with the MG was so successful and has given him such enjoyment, that he is now thinking in terms of the whole family, who have also become enthusiasts over the sports-car type of ride. The next blessed event at Doc Little's house will be the breathlessly awaited arrival of a 2½-liter Riley sedan —but that's another story.

In the meantime, if you are vaguely uneasy, have hot flashes when you hear a racing motor, become despondent when you look at that old crate in the garage, try Dr. Little's prescription: one sports car of your choice, plus the open road; mix well with discretion and careful driving; take this medicine as soon and as often as possible. Brother, if this doesn't cure that urge and make you a happy, healthy man, nothing will.

The twin S.U. carburetters, electric petrol pump and scuttle-mounted tool-box are all easy to reach.

The M.G. Type TD

IT was a very knowledgeable advertisement copywriter who first coined the slogan "Safety Fast" to describe the products of the M.G. Car Co., Ltd. It was apt in those far-off days and it certainly remains true to-day.

The safety of the driver of a car designed for high-speed cruising lies very much in his comfort and convenience. Such matters as the position of steering wheel, pedals, switches and instruments, as well as the degree of support provided by the driving seat itself, all contribute to the peace of mind of the conductor.

In these respects, the TD Midget scores all along the line. The leather-covered seats, the bench squab and the steering column are each adjustable, so that most types of the human species can make themselves quickly at home at the controls. We did find, however, that a gauntletted hand could produce a blast from the horns when feeling for the dipswitch; button and switch are grouped together in the centre of the facia panel.

The other aspects of safety at high speed concern steering, road-holding and braking. Here again, the latest M.G. Midget at once gives the driver a quite remarkable feeling of full control as soon as he takes the wheel. With the hood folded into the well behind the seats, all-round vision could hardly be bettered. The rack and pinion steering is precise, quick, and unusually light. Completely free from road shocks the steering wheel remains steady in the hands up to maximum speed and still manages to convey to the driver the comforting impression that he is not altogether divorced from the front wheels by complicated linkages.

The TD Midget in all-weather trim. Wide and low-built, its lines are solid and practical, suggesting the first-class road-holding of this thoroughbred.

familiar roads, it was very soon evident that the TD was one of those cars which enjoy being hustled along. There is some body roll and some oversteer, but neither characteristic is sufficient to induce instability.

The front end really does cling to the road, the rear can be safely slid and the roll can be ignored altogether. Changes of direction have to be very violent indeed to create tyre howl and it would seem that the occasion just does not arise when the driver has to "fight the wheel." Steering is a matter of gentle thumb and wrist pressure, rather than wide elbow movements.

The 1,250 c.c. o.h.v. engine is high revving, remarkably willing and flexible. Much of the pleasure of driving the TD lies in keeping the revs. up and to this end the designers have provided a four-speed gearbox which is a delight to use. The remote-control lever is where it should be—above the prop. shaft and below the left hand.

During the period in which the Midget was in our keeping, we were able to cover

several hundreds of miles, all of them pleasurably, but none more so than those over winding B-class roads. It is on such roads as these, with their straights which are never quite straight and their endless succession of corners of varying degree, that the TD is at its most stimulating.

The car reaches 60 m.p.h. in third gear very rapidly indeed, and, in favourable circumstances, 80 m.p.h. in top. Cruising effortlessly at between 65 and 70 m.p.h. neither engine nor driver show sign of fatigue, even at the end of a long day on the road. Moreover, at a steady 40 m.p.h. we achieved a petrol consumption figure of 39 m.p.g. which is no mean performance.

Within the obvious limitations imposed by folding hood and detachable sidescreens, the M.G. is a comfortable winter car. There is some drumming and flapping from the hood when erected; nor is it to be expected that this type of body is entirely draught-free. To the enthusiast these things count for little and Monte Carlo Rally weather is mercifully short.

The TD M.G. was designed for enthusiasts who know what they want. It has speed—and works-recommended "mods" produce much more—it has excellent road-holding and zest in every gear. Leisurely and smooth in traffic, it is crisp, invigorating and absolutely safe on the open road.

Front suspension of the TD is vastly different from its predecessors in that it is independent, using helical springs and wishbones of unequal length. Semi-elliptic springs are used at the rear, but the chassis members are upswept over the axle. Firm

IN BRIEF

Engine.—4-cyl., o.h.v. 66.5 mm. by 90 mm. (1,250 c.c.), 54.5 b.h.p. at 5,500 r.p.m. Twin S.U. inclined carburetters. S.U. electric petrol pump. Compression ratio, 7.25 to 1.

Transmission.—Clutch, Borg and Beck 7¼-in. single dry-plate. Hardy Spicer propeller shaft. Gears, 5.125, 7.098, 10.609 (synchromesh) and 17.938 to 1. Reverse, 17.938 to 1. Rear axle, hypoid bevel.

General.—Suspension: front, independent (helical springs and wishbones); rear, semi-elliptic. Shock absorbers, Luvax Girling hydraulic. Brakes, Lockheed, 9-in. drums, 2LS at front. Tyres, Dunlop, 5.50 by 15 E.L.P. Electrical equipment, Lucas, 12-volt, c.v.c.

Dimensions, etc.—Length, 12 ft. 1 in.; width, 4 ft. 10⅜ in.; wheelbase, 7 ft. 10 in.; clearance, 6 in.; turning circle, 31½ ft.; turns of wheel from lock to lock, 2½; weight unladen, 18 cwt.

Performance.—Touring maximum (measured quarter-mile after three-quarter-mile run), 77.65 m.p.h. Speeds in gears, 21 m.p.h. (first), 41 m.p.h. (second), 60 m.p.h. (third). Acceleration, 0—50 m.p.h. (through the gears), 14.1 secs., 20—40 m.p.h. (top gear), 11.5 secs., 30—50 m.p.h., 12.1 secs., 40—60 m.p.h., 14.9 secs. Gradient climbable in top, 1 in 11.7. Petrol consumption (40 m.p.h. cruising), 39.2 m.p.g.

Price.—£530 plus £295 18s. 11d. purchase tax (£825 18s. 11d.).

Manufacturers.—The M.G. Car Co., Ltd. (Sales Division), Cowley, Oxford.

front and rear damping is furnished by Luvax Girling hydraulic shock absorbers.

This combination of light, definite steering and relatively soft suspension is one of the most attractive features of the car. After a number of tentative essays in cornering on

Individual seats, squab and steering column are adjustable. Luggage is carried in the well behind the seats.

just for YOU

EXCLUSIVELY MG,

THESE ITEMS MAY BE

JUST WHAT YOU'RE

LOOKING FOR

With SEVERAL THOUSAND MGs touring the highways of the United States, we thought that many owners would like to see some of the many accessories available to them. Some of these you have seen in advertisements, others are completely new and have not been released for sale as yet. Some of the items are strictly "doll up" types but others are functional and practical, adding much to your MG driving pleasure.

It is impossible to list every accessory that is being manufactured as there are many small shops that have designed a small item sold mainly to, and for the benefit of, their customers on the local market. The items on these pages are available through national distribution, either by MG agencies or by mail.

There are many tops for the MG, but the newest sensation is this Fiberglas coupe-type affair. It is easily attachable with a pair of clips and has been quite successful on the West Coast

A tinted sun visor will greatly increase the driving pleasure of the MG owner who lives in the Southwest. It clips on the top of the windshield without marring the frame or interfering with the top.

A gimmick that William Orr of Los Angeles built to avoid the "kidney punch" that the wind can give, is this light plastic shield that fits into the side curtain mounting brackets. It does a good job, while not interfering with the opening of the doors

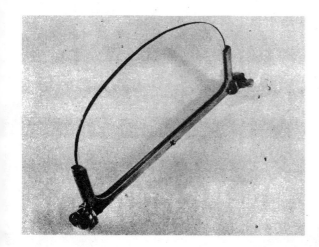

For the competition enthusiast, the genuine "Brooklands" type sports shield is now available. These act as deflectors more than as actual shields and are mounted with two permanently attached posts (not shown). In this manner, the shield may be removed for windshield-up operation, but may be easily re-installed for competition

Windwings are available in several models. All of them do a good job of keeping the wind blast from the side of your face. If you do much long distance driving, these are musts. They also fold back against the cowl when the side curtains are in place. In addition there are other types that may be removed and used as sports shields when the windshield is folded down flat

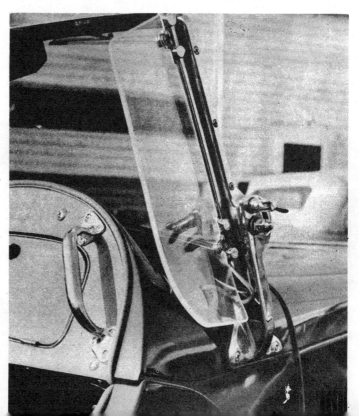

A wheel for the TD model is this one with a laminated wood rim and a two-bar stainless steel frame. The wheel is flexible, but not to the point of giving a "soft" feel

While on the subject of steering wheels, the center medallion, depicted above, is a good-looking dress-up item. Up to the present time, it is available only for TD models

The genuine Bluemel's "Brooklands" wheel is now available in this country in several colors. This is an extremely good-looking accessory for the MG and its 17-inch diameter somewhat aids the handling qualities

Another type of wheels just put on the market are these good-looking and reasonably priced gadgets for the TD

*Directional signals may not be an absolute necessity,
but they are attractive and convenient.
Easily installed on the TD, they are amber-colored
with a bulb powerful enough to be seen
at a great distance, even in bright sunlight*

*If you own a TC and are suffering from a worn
steering, or one that binds, this steering kit with
its roller action is a sure remedy.
Many of the competition TCs are fitted with this kit*

*One of the best dress-up items (above) for the TD
is a set of wheel disks. Although most of the
American "custom" disks may be fitted to the MG,
these are made just for the TD
and are louvered to aid brake cooling*

*If you like wheels, these (above left)
are just about the ultimate in good looks.
Made in Italy under license from Rudge, they come
with plated steel or buffed alloy rims and spokes*

*In combination with wheel disks (left),
or with a plain stock wheel, these new, cast aluminum
dummy "knock offs" may be just what you are
looking for. They are supplied with the MG insert
in the center of the hub and attach
to the stock hub cap with two screws from the rear*

Luggage racks for the MG are very popular
in Europe and are becoming
more and more popular here. This is
one type that fits above the fuel tank
and carries the baggage high

Along with the tonneau covers, a tire cover
of matching fabric presents a most attractive appearance.
They are available for either the TC or TD
from national distributors,
or may be custom-made by your local top shop

Tonneau covers are probably
the largest-selling accessories
made for the MG. Many of them are
ready-made, but others have
been tailored to the individual's
taste. In any case, they are
an extremely practical item
for your sports car

49

This is another type of luggage carrier that folds up against the spare when not in use. It carries the bags low, but away to the rear when traveling

Another new item that is meeting with considerable success in the competition field is a new Fiberglas front fender for the TD models. Lighter than the aluminum fender, it is good-looking and is supplied in prime coat ready to paint any color desired

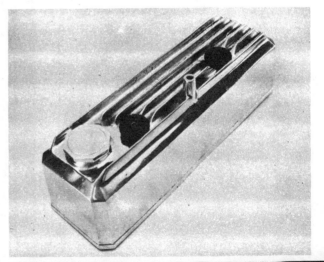

MG oil filters (above) have been worth their weight in gold in most sections of the country. However, there is a replacement filter being made domestically for all MG models that utilizes a standard American cartridge

For those who like fins on a valve cover (above right), here is a brand new item for the under-hood area. Also of polished aluminum, it is heavy enough to deaden all but the wildest tappets

For the clean engine enthusiast, here is a buffed aluminum rocker-arm cover (right) that silences the valves considerably and dresses up the engine

Without the arm rest comes this brake cover to prevent the wife from covering her skirt with the cable lubricant. It is provided in matching or contrasting materials and simply snaps around the handle

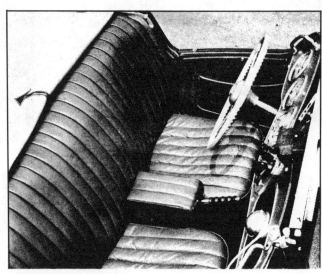

Here is still another type of arm rest for the TD that serves as a brake cover and helps to keep the right people on the right side of the car

Another, and very handy, arrangement (above) is this combined ashtray and center arm rest. It does not interfere with the operation of the shift lever and keeps the ashes off the floor and out of the driver's eyes

To better aid the Forestry Service in fire prevention, there is a very neat, in-the-door ashtray rig (above left) on the market. The outer bowl is easily removable for cleaning and the gadget is located right where the driver needs it

For entertainment when you travel (left), you will enjoy this Philco set built into your driveshaft tunnel. It does not interfere with shifting, or with the transmission filler plug

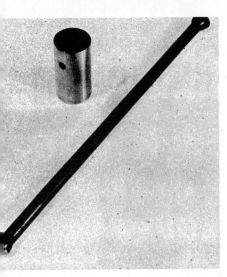

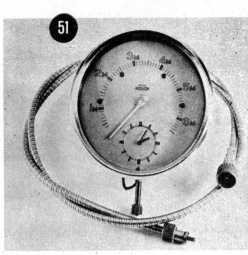

For the racing MG owner, this tubular push-rod and special tappet will considerably lighten the valve train. On more recent models the oil hole has been relocated for better lubrication at all speeds

Although the latest TDs are equipped with an engine (water) temperature gauge, this unit is available for the earlier models. Designed to fit into the radiator fitting, it is easily installed and the Stewart-Warner gauge may be mounted in or under the instrument panel

If you are having trouble with your speedometer, the cable breaks, or the noise bothers you, you might try this Stewart-Warner conversion. Made by an enthusiast, it uses all-American components behind the face. It is available for both TCs and TDs

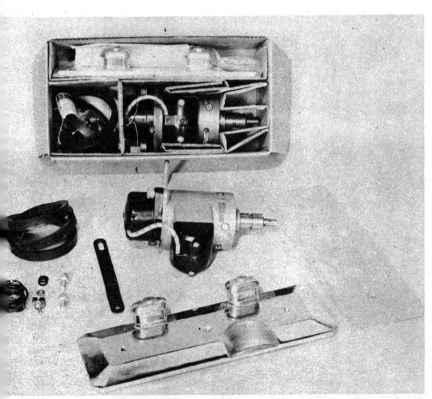

If you like to carry around a lot of small, but valuable items and are always worrying about their safety, this locking tonneau cover is just about the ticket

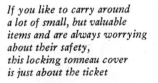

Engine accessories are a book unto themselves, but here is one that has been quite successful. It is a Lucas magneto kit with all necessary parts for installation including a valve side plate with breather openings

PERFORMIN

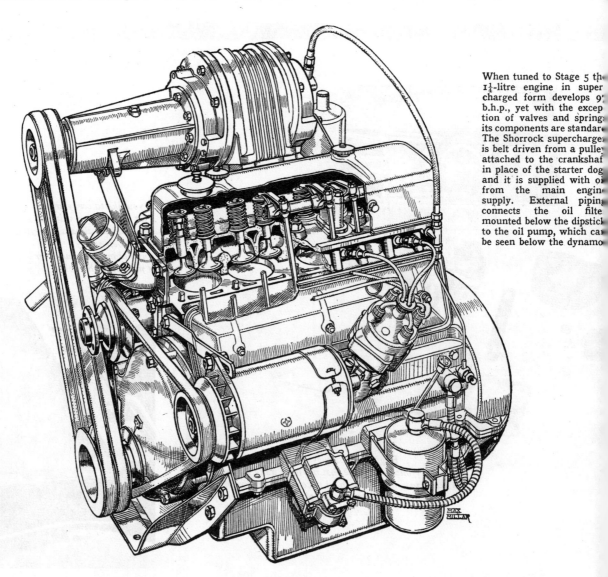

The car used for these tests was a production
TD M.G. Midget.

THE M.G. Midget is a car that has had a very long and successful life, and in one or other of its many forms it has been owned, loved and longed for by a large number of people interested in motoring. In the various forms in which it has appeared since its introduction its character and general conception have remained unchanged. However, many detail changes have been made through the years in the interests of performance, comfort and economy. During this process the car has, to a certain extent, grown up. For example, the power unit has a capacity of 1,250 c.c. compared with 847 c.c. at the beginning, in 1929. The present model, known as the TD, also has independent front suspension and two leading shoe brakes, to name only two chassis features. Although the body is now larger it still retains the family likeness of its ancestors, and the car n easily mistaken for any other *marque*.

In view of its popularity, and the type of owner for whic it is designed, there is no doubt that where several M.C owners are gathered together the subject of the performanc of their respective cars will be freely discussed.

The question of tuning for increased performance is o on which much has been said, and is something that can lea to either success or disappointment. In either case it likely to be costly in both time and money. With this i mind the M.G. company have very wisely carried out considerable amount of development work to guide th owner in his quest for improved performance. Brief detai of a number of different tuning stages have been listed i

When tuned to Stage 5 th $1\frac{1}{4}$-litre engine in super charged form develops 9 b.h.p., yet with the excep tion of valves and spring its components are standar The Shorrock supercharge is belt driven from a pulle attached to the crankshaf in place of the starter dog and it is supplied with oi from the main engin supply. External pipin connects the oil filte mounted below the dipstick to the oil pump, which ca be seen below the dynamo

IDGETS

M.G.   By John Rabson

booklet issued by the manufacturers, called *Tuning for M.G. Midget Engines.*

Now, it must be pointed out that although the manufacturers are in a position to say what should be done, and also to supply the special components required for some of the stages, *they are not able to supply new cars in a tuned form or to tune owners' cars,* as this would, of course, interfere with normal production. However, if it is known what to do and what not to do there is a good chance of success. More important even than this, perhaps, is a clear idea of what the ultimate result is likely to be when the tuning is finished. Consequently, *The Autocar* has, over a period of several months, exhaustively road tested a TD M.G. in its various tuning stages from standard production to Stage 5.

Before any tuning is attempted it must be decided for what purpose the car is required; also—and this will to a certain extent be inter-related with the first consideration—what type of fuel is available to run it on. The fuel question is of vital importance, and until this has been decided very little tuning of any kind can be done. Each type and blend of fuel has what is known as a highest useful compression ratio; therefore, unless the octane rating of the fuel will permit, there is no point in increasing the compression ratio, which is one of the best-known methods of increasing performance. Another method of increasing engine output is by supercharging, which may also in some cases be accompanied by an increase in compression ratio. Apart from the fundamental changes of the type mentioned, there are two other ways of improving engine performance. One is to reduce the friction between the moving parts, and the other is to improve the volumetric efficiency or breathing. These two items are not brought about by any form of magic, but by hard work and skilful use of tools, much patience, a basic knowledge of what can be done and cannot be done, and still more hard work.

Making the Most of the Power

A stage-by-stage treatment of the engine will be given later, but before this is done there are other aspects of the tuning that must be considered. Briefly, the performance of a car depends on the power required relative to the power that is available. Now, assuming that the total weight is not affected much during the tuning, and also that the body shape remains unchanged, the curve showing the power required to drive the car will remain the same.

To determine the required overall gear ratio it is necessary to have a knowledge of both the power required and the power available if the best overall performance is to be obtained. If the gear ratio has been determined for a car powered by an engine that develops, say, 54 b.h.p., as in the standard TD M.G., it is obvious that if the power output is increased to any marked degree some modification to the overall gear ratio will be required. If this is not done the engine will have exceeded its maximum safe working speed in r.p.m. before the maximum speed is reached corresponding to the power available. This means that for a given car, if the b.h.p. is increased the m.p.h. per 1,000 r.p.m. of the engine on top gear must also be increased, and to do this the gear ratio must be lowered [Thus providing a higher gear.—Ed.] or a similar effect produced, for example, by fitting larger diameter tyres to the rear wheels.

Modifications made to the axle ratio on the M.G. are listed in Table I, and a graph shows the effect on the performance

To prevent fuel starvation, scuttle mounted twin fuel pumps were used on Stages 1 to 4. Both fuel pumps supply both the carburettors. For Stage 5 a special fuel pump is attached close to the fuel tank, and extra large diameter pipes are used to convey the fuel to the float chamber.

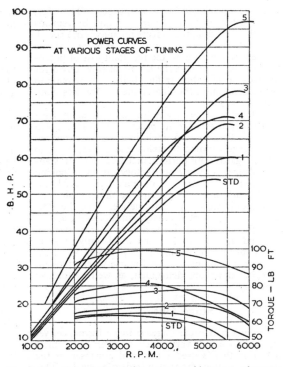

The five tuning stages enable a very wide range of power output figures to be obtained. It will be noticed that the power output for Stage 2 (9.3 to 1 compression ratio unblown) is almost the same as the power obtained in Stage 4 with a supercharger and low compression ratio engine.

At Stage 4 of the tuning a Shorrock supercharger is fitted to the engine running on standard compression ratio. Twin fuel pumps feed the single S.U. carburettor mounted low down at the back of the supercharger.

PERFORMING MIDGETS . . . . . continued

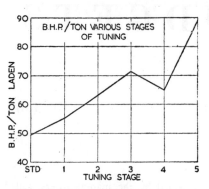

The b.h.p. per ton figure of the TD Midget varied with the tuning stages as shown in this graph.

DATA

PRICE (basic), with 2-seater body, £530
British purchase tax, £295 18s 11d.
Total (in Great Britain), £825 18s 11d.

ENGINE : Capacity : 1,250 c.c. (76.28 cu in).
Number of cylinders : 4.
Bore and stroke : 66.5 × 90 mm (2.62 × 3.54in).
Valve gear : O.h.v.

WEIGHT (with 5 gals fuel), 18½ cwt (2,030 lb).
Weight distribution (per cent) 49.3 F ; 50.7 R.
Laden as tested : 22 cwt (2,444 lb).
Lb per c.c. (laden) : !.96

BRAKES : Type : F, 2 leading shoe. R, Leading and trailing.
Method of operation : F Hydraulic. R Hydraulic.
Drum dimensions : F 9in diameter, 1½in wide. R 9in diameter, 1½in wide.
Lining area : F 49.74 sq in. R 49.74 sq in (91.2 sq in per ton laden).

*TYRES : 5.50—15in.
Pressures (lb per sq in) : 18 F ; 18 R (normal).

TANK CAPACITY : 12.5 Imperial gallons.
Oil sump, 9 pints.
Cooling system, 12 pints.

TURNING CIRCLE : 31ft 3in (L and R)
Steering wheel turns (lock to lock) : 2¾.

DIMENSIONS : Wheelbase 7ft 10in.
Track : 3ft 11⅜in (F) ; 4ft 2in (R).
Length (overall) : 12ft 1in.
Height : 4ft 5in.
Width 4ft 10⅜in.
Ground clearance : 6in.
Frontal area : 16.6 sq ft (approx, with hood up. 13.5 sq ft, with aero screen).

ELECTRICAL SYSTEM : 12-volt. 51 ampère-hour battery.
Head lights : Single dip, 36-36 watt.

SUSPENSION : Front, independent, wishbones and coil springs.
Rear, half-elliptic.

* 6.00 — 15in tyres used for Stage 5.

---

in the indirect ratios produced by these changes. The effect of weight is important in tuning, but it should be remembered that it is the total drag that affects the maximum speed, and the weight that affects acceleration. However, if the weight is not kept to a minimum the resultant loss of potential acceleration may mean that the car must slow down for a corner or because of other traffic, before its maximum speed is ever reached; also, the lighter the car the less work there is for the brakes.

The car used for these tests was first submitted in standard trim. It was put through its paces, and, in fact, given the normal Road Test routine, including several hundred miles of normal road running to enable the driver to get to know the car as regards both performance and feel. In standard trim the Midget is a very satisfactory car. On looking back, after having driven it when its maximum speed was around the 100 mark, it would perhaps be thought slow by those interested only in sheer performance. Yet the ultimate maximum speed is not the only consideration, and in standard form the car recorded a mean maximum speed of 72.5 m.p.h., and this from an engine of only 1¼-litre capacity. On Pool fuel the engine is very smooth and flexible, so that the car is quite suitable for use when frequent stops and slowing down are demanded, as well as for fast open-road cruising.

Stage One

Perhaps the most noticeable increase in performance, yet one that keeps the car still very much an everyday vehicle as opposed to one that is used for special purposes, is the initial tuning modifications from standard to Stage 1. This is a simple tune-up and consists of raising the compression ratio to 8.6 by 1 (by means of machining ³⁄₃₂in off the cylinder head face), polishing out the ports, fitting larger valves and

consequently stronger valve springs, and replacing the 1.25in diameter twin S.U. carburettors with 1.5in diameter components, fed by the twin fuel pumps. Modifications to the chassis consisted of lowering the axle ratio from 5.125 to 4.875 to 1 and fitting an extra set of dampers. Also, purely for the personal comfort of the driver, who was not in favour of driving with the windscreen flat with air temperatures around freezing point, a glass plate type of de-froster unit was fitted to the windscreen.

The first impression on driving the car in Stage 1 form was the very considerable increase in liveliness that it has, and under test conditions this impression was confirmed. The maximum speed was increased by 5 m.p.h. and there was also a marked improvement in the acceleration figures through the gears. Acceleration times in one gear from constant speeds, however, were, generally speaking, longer. Now this fact is interesting as it shows one of the fundamental things about tuning that is sometimes overlooked; that is, as the top end performance is increased, the bottom end power and consequently some of the flexibility also are often lost. For example, if the valve throat diameter is increased to improve the breathing at the top end the gas speed at low engine speeds will be reduced. This means that the pulling power and flexibility at low speeds on top gear will perhaps not be very good, and in consequence more use of the indirect gears must be made. In turn this may result in an increased fuel consumption. This trend can be seen throughout the whole of the tests, and confirms a phrase in the tuning book, " Power costs Money."

Now although there is a very definite gain in performance this is not obtained without some loss in smoothness. However, it must be remembered that at this stage the car is still running on Pool fuel. During the tests some pinking was noticed, but this can be reduced to a minimum by using the indirect gears and not letting the engine slog away at low

TABLE I: BRIEF TUNING DATA FOR VARIOUS STAGES

	Comp. Ratio	Carburettors	Carburettor Needles	Plugs	Valves	Valve Springs (fitted load lb)	B.H.P. at specified r.p.m.	Axle Ratio	M.P.H. per 1,000 r.p.m.	Supercharge pressure	Fuel
Standard	7.25 to 1	Two × 1.1/4″	ES. ×0.090″	L.10.S	Std.	120	54 at 5200	5.125 to 1	14.42	—	Pool
Stage 1	8.6 to 1	Two × 1.1/2″	LS1. ×0.090″	L.10.S.	Large	150	60 at 5600	4.875 to 1	15.195	—	Pool
Stage 2	9.3 to 1	Two × 1.1/2″	RLS. ×0.090″	L.10.S.	Large	150	69 at 5500	4.875 to 1	15.195	—	50 per cent alcohol
Stage 3	12.0 to 1	Two × 1.1/2″	VE. ×0.125″	R.49	Large	150	78 at 5750	4.55 to 1	16.259	—	80 per cent alcohol
Stage 4	7.25 to 1	One × 1.1/2″	RA. ×0.100″	L.10.S	Std.	120	71 at 5500	4.875 to 1	15.195	6 lb sq in	80 octane lead free
Stage 5	9.3 to 1	One × 1.3/4″	RM7.×0.1875″	R.49	Large	150	97 at 6000	4.55 to 1	17.00	6 lb sq in	85 per cent alcohol

speed on top gear. The car is quite happy in city traffic generally, yet it should be recorded that on one occasion only, in very dense slow-moving traffic, it did show signs of getting hot. On all other occasions, including fast main road and hilly journeys, as well as during the actual performance testing, no trouble of this kind was experienced. With the extra set of spring dampers fitted the car has a much firmer ride at high speeds at the cost of some increased vibration over rough surfaces at low speed.

For Stage 2 the compression ratio is further increased to 9.3 to 1 by machining a total of 0.125in off the cylinder head, which is the absolute maximum that can safely be removed. As in Stage 1, large valves are used, and the twin 1½in bore S.U. carburettors were tuned to suit the 50 per cent alcohol fuel. At this stage the engine develops 69 b.h.p. at 5,500 r.p.m. as compared with 54 b.h.p. at 5,200 r.p.m. when in standard form, or 60 b.h.p. at 5,600 r.p.m. with the Stage 1 tuning. Compared with Stage 1, perhaps the most noticeable thing about the behaviour is the very considerable increase in smoothness, yet the gain in maximum speed is not nearly as marked for the 9 b.h.p. increase as it is between the standard engine and Stage 1 for an increase of only 6 b.h.p. This is, of course, brought about by the shape of the

Even though the power output was almost doubled at Stage 5 compared with the untuned production engine, standard crankshaft and connecting rods were used. Note the clamping bolts in the split little-end eyes.

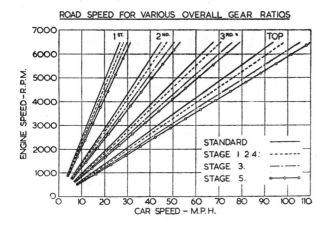

This graph shows the road speed corresponding to the engine speed for the various gear ratios used during the tests.

power required curve, and shows the effect of wind resistance as the speed is increased. The acceleration figures from a standing start through the gears show an overall improvement; accelerations on one gear from constant speeds are slightly worse. The fuel consumption is considerably increased, but this is not surprising, because of its high alcohol content. It is possible to run in this stage of tune on 80 octane fuel. This would enable the car to be used for normal running in countries where this type of fuel is available. Both Stages 3 and 5 of the tuning are intended for competition use only, and will therefore be dealt with together later.

Adding a Blower

Next, then, we come to Stage 4, which consists of supercharging the engine in standard form, but using the 4.875 to 1 axle ratio (as fitted in Stages 1 and 2). In this form the engine is blown at 6 lb per sq in by means of a Shorrock supercharger, which is belt driven from the engine crankshaft, and for this stage it is fed by a single 1.5in S.U. carburettor. For test purposes 80 octane lead-free aviation fuel was used, although it is possible to run on 70 octane fuel, at the expense of a slight reduction in output. In the past there has been perhaps a feeling that when a car is supercharged it at once becomes messy, unreliable, and likely to blow up at the slightest provocation. This may have been true in the past, when some of the problems connected with supercharging were not fully understood, but it certainly does not apply to the Stage 4 M.G.

The general improvement in filling and distribution brought about by the blower results in an overall improve-

ment in performance as regards both maximum speed and acceleration compared with Stage 2. On the other hand, the fact that it does not have such a good bottom end as the standard engine is reflected by the acceleration figures from a constant 10 and 20 m.p.h. on top gear. It must be remembered that the change in axle ratio will affect the result slightly. However, compared with the general improvement in performance this effect is of little moment, as a driver could overcome it by use of the gears, yet it does show what is perhaps the major difficulty in tuning; that is, to obtain an overall increase in power output without losing the bottom end or engine flexibility. In this supercharged form the car is quite suitable for normal road use, but the fuel consumption is, of course, increased as compared with the unblown engine; also, as the oil supply for the supercharger is taken from the engine, the sump must be replenished more frequently than when the engine is unblown. The supercharger is quiet in operation. In fact, it is not until the engine is really starting to rev that the familiar whine is heard at all. No difficulty in starting from cold was experienced.

The stages dealt with so far cover tuning suitable for a car that is used to some extent as a normal road vehicle. In the next issue the two remaining stages will be considered that are intended purely for competition work and not suitable for normal use. General impressions and results will also be discussed.

To be concluded

For all stages of tuning (from Stage 1) an extra set of dampers was fitted. This view shows the Andrex unit fitted to the front suspension. The gaiter for the rack and pinion steering can be clearly seen.

by John Rabson

The external appearance of the car remains the same except for Stage 5, when oversized tyres are fitted at the rear. Owing to the cooling effect of the alcohol fuel used for these last two stages it is necessary to blank off a portion of the radiator to keep up the engine temperature. This was done by placing another aluminium sheet in front of the grille.

PERFORMING MIDGETS

Part 2: Concluding the Report on Stage by Stage Tuning of a TD M.G.

SOME of the general problems connected with tuning have been considered, together with results obtained with those stages that are suitable for normal road operation if the correct grade of fuel is available. To complete the picture there remain two further stages which are really suitable only for competition work, although during tests the car was driven on the road in both these conditions for a considerable distance.

At Stage 3 the car has the character and, perhaps, the temperament of a racer. This is not surprising, as the engine now has a compression ratio of 12 to 1 obtained by using a cylinder head of standard dimensions in conjunction with special pistons. Large diameter valves are, of course, fitted, and the 80 per cent alcohol fuel is metered by twin 1½in S.U. carburettors. At this stage starting from cold is best performed with the aid of a rope and a tender car, unless there happens to be a team of strong men available to push. However, once the engine is warm starting can easily be performed with the standard starter motor, and in such circumstances, during the test, the response was almost instantaneous. With 78 b.h.p. at 5,750 r.p.m. now available, it is necessary to change the rear axle ratio to 4.55 to 1 to

From this graph it can be seen how the various tuning stages tend to improve the maximum performance at the expense of top gear flexibility. On the 10-30 m.p.h. graph for example, at Stage 5 no top gear acceleration could be recorded. On the other hand, at this speed range it was possible to obtain figures on first gear without over-revving the engine.

The curve below is a graphical representation of the acceleration times from a standing start through the gears at the various tuning stages.

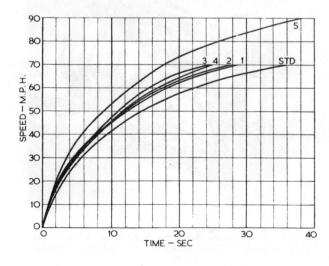

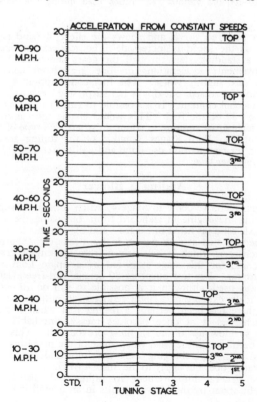

For Stage 3 (12 to 1 compression ratio) large twin S.U. carburettors are used. These are supplied with fuel by the twin electric fuel pumps mounted on the scuttle, piped so that both pumps supply both carburettors. This is necessary to prevent possible starvation of fuel, as the excessive temperature caused by a weak mixture could produce extreme overheating.

make effective use of the new-found top end power without over-revving the engine. These modifications produce an increase in maximum speed of 3 m.p.h. compared with Stage 4. They also give a noticeable improvement in the acceleration times from a standing start through the gears, in spite of the change in axle ratio. On the other hand, acceleration times on any one gear do not show any improvement; in fact, they are, if anything, slightly worse.

The car is very pleasant to drive at this stage provided that the lack of bottom end flexibility compared with that available with the engine in standard form is remembered, and the car driven accordingly. It is also very important to maintain the correct engine temperature, as the cool running qualities of the alcohol fuel can, in certain circum-

TRACTIVE EFFORT

	STAGE 2 Pull lb per ton	Gradient	STAGE 3 Pull lb per ton	Gradient	STAGE 4 Pull lb per ton	Gradient	STAGE 5 Pull lb per ton	Gradient
Top	175	1 in 13	156	1 in 14	205	1 in 11	245	1 in 9.5
3rd	270	1 in 8.4	273	1 in 8.2	293	1 in 7.7	248	1 in 6.5
2nd	400	1 in 5.5	411	1 in 5.3	411	1 in 5.3	495	1 in 4.5

TRACTIVE RESISTANCE lb per ton at 10 m.p.h.

STAGE 2	STAGE 3	STAGE 4	STAGE 5*
10	40	16.7	15

BRAKES

EFFICIENCY	PEDAL PRESSURE (lb)
84.5 per cent	102
79.6 per cent	50

stances, cause over-cooling, which may result in lumpy running at low speeds, accompanied by some hesitation when the throttle is opened. During this test, which was carried out at an air temperature of 59 deg F, it was found necessary further to blank off the radiator for the acceleration tests in constant gears, although for other tests the single aluminium sheet fitted, as shown in one of the photographs, was entirely satisfactory. Mixture strength is of the utmost importance at this stage, as any weakness could easily cause overheating, which could have very serious results. Under normal conditions, this would not happen, but a temporary starvation could take place if the car were driven with only a very small quantity of fuel in the tank, and fuel

movement during rapid cornering, for example, permitted air to enter one of the fuel lines. It is therefore advisable to keep a considerable quantity of fuel in the tank to eliminate this possibility.

The final test in this group is Stage 5, which consists of the 9.3 to 1 compression ratio engine, supercharged at 6lb per sq in by means of a Shorrock blower. As in Stage 3, the car is fitted with the 4.55 to 1 rear axle ratio, but over-sized tyres are used to give 17 m.p.h. per 1,000 r.p.m. engine speed, compared with 16.258 m.p.h. per 1,000 r.p.m. for Stage 3 with 5.50—15in tyres. With 97 b.h.p. available under the bonnet, the little TD really does go like a bomb, and when driven on the road it has been responsible for a number of puzzled expressions on the faces of drivers in cars that it has passed, and who did not know that the car was tuned. Considering the type of body, which does not cheat the wind as well as some, the maximum speed of 96 m.p.h. (approximately 1 m.p.h. per b.h.p.), with the hood and side screens in position, is very good. It can be further increased

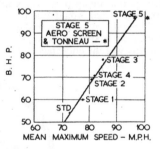

This curve shows the mean maximum speed obtained under test conditions relative to the engine b.h.p.

to just over the 100 mark if the car is fitted with a full tonneau cover and an aero screen. What it would do with a full streamline body must be left to the imagination, or to Goldie Gardner.

Normal racing car drill must be performed as regards plug changing at Stage 5. Often the engine could be started from cold by the normal starter motor, although this was difficult at times and the towing method had to be used. Starting from hot could be easily performed at all times with the starter. Because of its potential maximum speed this Stage 5 test was carried out in Belgium on the Jabbeke motor road.

On the road itself, which is excellently surfaced, the car

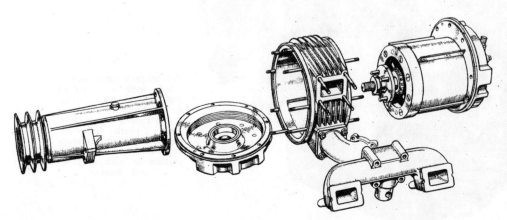

An exploded view showing the mechanism of the eccentric vane type supercharger fitted to the M.G. engine. The inlet elbow is arranged to suit the three-bolt flange on the large carburettor used for Stage 5. In the centre of the inlet manifold at the bottom is the super-charger blow-off valve. Lubrication is provided by oil piped from the engine to the union that can be seen behind the rear end-plate of the supercharger.

ran very well indeed. However, on some of the smaller roads leading off the main highway the *pavé* is very uneven, and on these surfaces some irregularity in running was noticed, but this stopped again as soon as the car returned to a smooth road. This is interesting, and may have been caused by frothing of the alcohol, the condition being accentuated by the firmness of the suspension when fitted with the additional dampers. Under normal conditions the standard clutch was quite satisfactory in dealing with the much increased power output, yet under the strenuous conditions of the repeated standing start acceleration tests slip was experienced, but only at this stage.

There are a number of points that arise from an examination of the results of these tests. First, before any tuning is undertaken at all it must be decided for what purpose the car is required. There is absolutely no point in tuning for its own sake with no ultimate aim in view; also an engine should not be tuned more than is necessary to give the desired result, as this would only unduly stress the components and also increase the fuel bill. Perhaps one of the things that is most noticeable is the way that engine flexibility at the bottom end is lost as the top end power output is increased. This loss, of course, can be compensated for by modifications in driving methods, which will result in an overall gain in performance, but again this will mean increased fuel consumption. This is perhaps best illustrated by reference to the graphs showing acceleration times on any one gear, and from rest through the gears.

It will be seen that as the tuning proceeds it is possible to make the car go progressively more quickly if the gears are used. On the other hand, if the gears are not used the acceleration times from, say, 10 to 30 m.p.h. on top gear will get longer as the tuning proceeds, until at Stage 5, for example, the car tested would not run satisfactorily below a speed of 25 m.p.h. on top gear, with the result that no figures on this gear at a speed below 30 m.p.h. were recorded. However, this was the only stage at which acceleration times

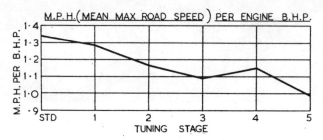

From this graph it can be seen that as the speed rises more and more horse-power is required to overcome wind resistance. For example, the standard engine enables a speed of approximately 1.34 m.p.h. per b.h.p. to be obtained, whereas at Stage 5 not better than 0.99 m.p.h. per b.h.p. is achieved.

for speeds of 70-90 m.p.h. on top gear could be recorded. This again emphasizes the fact that as the power available at the top end is increased by tuning, flexibility at low speeds is reduced. In other words, you cannot have it both ways. As the road speed increases the effect of wind resistance becomes more and more noticeable. This is illustrated in the graphs showing the m.p.h. per b.h.p. engine output. From these it can be seen that for the standard engine 54 b.h.p. gives a mean maximum speed of 72.5 m.p.h. An increase of 17 b.h.p. (to Stage 4) increases the mean maximum speed by only 9.5 m.p.h. Again, at Stage 5 the engine develops 97 b.h.p., which represents an increase of 43 over the standard engine; this 43 b.h.p. results in an increase in maximum road speed of 23.5 m.p.h. at the top end, most of this power being used in overcoming wind resistance. That is why for a given body style the increase from the standard to Stage 1, which results in a gain of 5 m.p.h. for 5 b.h.p., is not repeated in the same ratio farther up the range.

For Stage 5 the engine is fitted with a Shorrock supercharger and the cylinder head modified to give a 9.3 to 1 compression ratio. Twin V belts drive the supercharger and mixture is metered by a single S.U. carburettor with a three-bolt flange.

SPEEDS ON GEARS (M.P.H.)

	STD.	STAGE 1	STAGE 2	STAGE 3	STAGE 4	STAGE 5
Top ...	72.5 mean 75 best	77.5 79	80.75 81.5	85 90	82 86	96* 97*
3rd ...	50—60	50—64	42—64	60—72	60—71	58—72
2nd ...	30—40	30—42	30—40	40—46	35—44	40—47
1st ...	18—24	18—26	18—26	20—28	18—30	24—30

* Stage 5 with aero screen 100.5 mean and, with tonneau cover, 101 best

SPEEDOMETER CHECK (M.P.H.)

CAR SPEEDS		10	20	30	40	50	60	70	75	80	85	90	100
True Speed	Std.	11	20	31	41	51	61	71	75	—	—	—	—
	Stage 1, 2, and 4	10	21	30	40	50	60	70	—	80	—	—	—
	Stage 3	10.5	21	30	42	53	62	74	—	84	90	—	—
	Stage 5	12	23	32	42	52	61	70	—	79	—	89	99

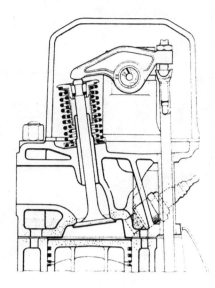

To obtain a compression ratio of 9.3 to 1 (as used in Stage 5) the cylinder head is machined to form a compact combustion chamber. A standard piston is used.

Stages 2 and 4 give rather similar results, and show two ways of obtaining somewhat similar outputs. Both the high compression ratio engine in Stage 2, and the supercharged standard compression ratio engine of Stage 4, can be driven on the road for normal transport with somewhat similar performance. What, then, should decide which arrangement of tuning should be used? For road operation the differences in output are not sufficiently great to be noticed under normal conditions. In fact, acceleration times through the gears from 0-50 m.p.h. are almost identical. However, above that speed the supercharged engine is at a slight advantage, though it is rather more thirsty than the unblown ver-

The left-hand piston is of the standard production type used for Stages 1, 2, 4 and 5, while on the right is the special piston used for Stage 3, which, in conjunction with a standard cylinder head, gives the compression ratio of 12 to 1.

sion. This is interesting, because Stage 2 is using a 50 per cent alcohol fuel, whereas the supercharged version (Stage 4) runs on 80 octane lead-free aviation spirit.

For competition purposes handicap arrangements would obviously tend to militate against the use of a supercharged engine in any other form than Stage 5, as both Stages 2 and 3 could produce results similar to or better than those from the supercharged version at Stage 4, without penalization from a competition angle. On the other hand, supercharging the engine according to Stage 4 does enable a very considerable increase in power output to be obtained with very little actual modification to the power unit, whereas the other stages require a number of internal modifications. It is therefore quite simple to convert the standard engine to Stage 4 and back to standard conditions again without obtaining a new or modified cylinder head, as would be required for most of the other stages. It must be remembered that modifica-

tions to the axle ratio are necessary to get the maximum output from the various stages of tuning.

To enable all stages of tuning to be carried out it is necessary to have at least three cylinder heads and two alternative sets of pistons, as well as three sizes of carburettor and special valve gear, and with these components available the M.G. can be tuned to suit a very wide number of requirements. The general design and the construction of the power unit as a whole are sufficiently robust to enable these large increases in power output to be obtained without fear of component failure or general lack of reliability. Yet it must be realized that, as the tuning is increased and the components become more highly stressed, so will the rate of wear and tendency towards unreliability be increased. This is only natural and does not reflect in any way on the design; in fact, it speaks very well indeed of the engine design when it is realized just how much power can be extracted from it without modifying the basic components such as the crankshaft or connecting rods, for example.

Obviously, any owner wishing to tune his car will have his own ideas as to how far he wishes to go, but, briefly, from the tests it would seem that Stage 1 tuning would suit the requirements of most people who want their Midgets to go rather faster than average without too much of an increase in the fuel bill. Stages 3 and 5 should be reserved for competition work only, while Stages 2 and 4 can be used for either road or competition work at the expense of an increased fuel consumption, and in a car used for road work, only provided that the correct type of fuel is readily available.

OVERALL FUEL CONSUMPTION

Overall fuel consumption at various tuning stages.

*A simple and attractive
color combination that is designed
to bring attention toward the forward
portion of the car, creating
an illusion of length. This is
a fairly common device that becomes
interesting when the upholstery is
dyed the same color as the paint trim.
The color separation may be
further accented by the use of
a stripe between the two colors.
A two-tone combination is
not recommended unless a very broad
separation stripe is to be used*

Painting Your MG

YOU CAN MAKE YOUR CAR LOOK LONGER
AND LOWER SAYS VINCE ALDRIN

IF YOU ARE planning to refinish your MG, here are some excellent suggestions offered by one of Southern California's outstanding paint stylists, Vince Aldrin, of Guild Auto Body. Vince is responsible for the very-good-looking red and bronze TD on this month's cover. When we asked him to tell us why so many people have brought their sports cars to him for color designing, Vince had the following to say:

"There is only one reason for painting an MG in a color design rather than in the normal process of refinishing. Many people want to change the general effect of the car by making it look longer, lower, or "just different." The four suggestions shown here tend to accomplish one or more of these things. In turn they can be modified by changing the type or color of a stripe, if a stripe is used. The color combinations may vary from a two tone creation of one color to full usage of sharply contrasting colors."

*Using the "spear" effect,
but with the top color lighter than
the lower color, length, and lowness
are accented. The color used on the
hood side panels is a tone
darker than the other two, fading
gradually into the door and
cowl panel. This is a rather difficult
thing to paint and is not recommended
for the home painter,
but its result is well worth the work*

A suggested color scheme for the TD owner who wishes he had more of the TC look. The sweep on the hood as well as the two-color fender treatment tend to narrow the width. From a side view, length has been gained by accentuating the fender line. Here is one situation in which strongly contrasting colors, or a subtle two-tone, can provide the desired effect

This is a version of the very popular "spear" effect. The foreign feeling is accentuated by bringing the cut-down door into full prominence. Again the illusion of length is given by the gradual taper of the painted design towards the radiator. The "spear" color is repeated under the fenders to show a definite contrast of the fender line and chassis. This is most effective when strongly contrasting colors are used

Goldie Gardner wipes the blood from his face as he walks away from the car after his accident ; a mechanic is carrying away the damaged right-side rear wheel spat.

RECORD-BREAKING M.G.

Goldie Gardner Once More Visits Utah : Alternative Power Units

WITH his famous streamlined M.G. record-breaking car, Lt.-Col. A. T. Gardner has once more been busy at Bonneville Salt Flats, Utah, U.S.A., and has captured several more international class records and a number of American national class records. Unfortunately, the surface of the famous salt lake was not in very good condition by reason of flooding, and on August 16, after taking several records in Class E (1,501-2,000 c.c.) the car got into a spin at 150 m.p.h. and demolished a marker post. The sign on top of the post fell on the plastic cockpit cover of the car, smashing it and cutting the driver's face slightly, while the engine of the car was damaged, and this put paid to any chances of further records in this category.

However, four days later Goldie went out again with the 1¼-litre engine installed, and although the conditions were still far from perfect he succeeded in capturing several short-distance records in Class F (1,101-1,500 c.c.). His full programme, nevertheless, had to be severely curtailed, but everyone will join in congratulating him on the successes achieved and in wishing him better luck next time.

Unlike some of Goldie Gardner's previous attempts when the capacity of the engine has been changed by removing some of the pistons from one basic engine, on this attempt two complete power units have been used. For Class E, a six-cylinder o.h.c. engine was used, while for the Class F runs, a modified M.G. TD unit provided the power. This second unit is similar to that described in *The Autocar* last year, and, very briefly, consists of a four-cylinder TD engine supercharged by means of one Shorrock blower which is shaft driven from the engine crankshaft. The engine is offset in the frame and consequently the differential unit is placed well to the left of the chassis longitudinal centre line. This enables the driver to sit very low and to the side of the transmission shaft instead of on top and astride it as would otherwise be necessary.

Wolseley-derived

For the Class E runs, a new six-cylinder power unit has been used and this will be described in some detail. The engine has not been designed, as it were, from a clean sheet, especially for the record attempt. That would be very desirable for those concerned technically, but much too costly for those concerned financially, as developing an engine of this type is a very expensive business indeed. However, a very good compromise was reached by selecting a likely looking power unit from the Nuffield range and modifying it to the extent necessary to make it suitable for its new job. Even if some completely new castings are used to suit the particular requirements of this type of engine, if some of the standard jigs and fixtures can be used during a number of the machining processes, a considerable saving in time and money results.

The cylinder block casting is similar in shape to that used on the Wolseley Six Eighty, from which the new unit was developed, but one of the essential differences is the arrangement of water passages between the cylinder block and head. It is part of the M.G. policy, where racing engines are concerned, to keep oil, water and mixture

International Class E (1,501 to 2,000 c.c.), standing start	
50 kilometres	143.23 m.p.h. (old record, 126.8)
50 miles	147.40 m.p h. (144.0)
100 kilometres	148.72 m.p.h. (128.1)

International Class F (1,101 to 1,500 c.c.), flying start	
5 miles	189.50 m.p.h. (139.2)
10 kilometres	182.84 m.p.h. (138.9)

American National Class E (1,501 to 2,000 c.c.), standing start	
25 kilometres	133.28 m.p.h.
25 miles	140.82 m.p.h.
50 kilometres	143.23 m.p.h.
50 miles	147.39 m.p.h.
75 kilometres	146.87 m.p.h.
100 kilometres	148.72 m.p.h.

Flying start	
25 kilometres	155.70 m.p.h.
25 miles	155.16 m.p.h.
50 kilometres	155.07 m.p.h.
50 miles	154.95 m.p.h.
75 kilometres	154.98 m.p.h.

American National Class F (1,101 to 1,500 c.c.), flying start	
1 kilometre	202.14 m.p.h.
1 mile	202.02 m.p.h.
5 kilometres	200.20 m.p.h.
5 miles	189.50 m.p.h.
10 kilometres	182.84 m.p.h.

(The above records are all subject to official confirmation).

as far apart as possible. Therefore, the new cylinder block is arranged to have no water passages through the cylinder head face, and so one gasket problem is solved. To enable the coolant to pass from the block to the head, external pipes are used.

The layout of the cooling circuit is, therefore, from the bottom of the radiator to the water pump (situated at the front of the engine and belt driven from a crankshaft pulley), from the water pump outlet to the front of the cylinder block, through the cylinder block, passing round all the bores and out at the rear of the block, through a transfer pipe and into the back of the cylinder head. It is then directed forward to cool all the valves, finally leaving the cylinder head at the front. From the front of the head the coolant is piped back to the radiator header tank which is mounted on the scuttle. The return pipe from the bottom of the header tank is connected to the top of the radiator, to complete the circuit. To prevent the possibility of core plugs in the block or head blowing out they are secured by bolted-on straps.

Stroke Reduction

To produce an engine of under 2-litre capacity the stroke has been reduced by 9.5 mm. The dimensions are 73.5 mm bore and 77.5 mm stroke, which gives a capacity of 1,973 c.c. compared with 2,215 c.c. for the standard engine with a 73.5 by 87 mm bore and stroke.

The reduction in stroke has been brought about by the use of a special crankshaft. This component was produced by Laystall and is dimensionally the same as the production crankshaft except for the shorter stroke. It runs in four main bearings which are of the

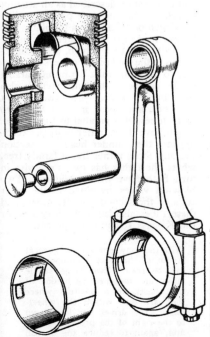

An exploded view of the piston, connecting rod, and fully floating gudgeon pin.

steel-backed white metal variety, as also are the big-end bearings. Not unnaturally, in an engine of this type, where the output is very much above that produced by the standard engine, and also because of the modified stroke, special connecting rods are used. As can be seen from the illustrations, these are of a very sturdy design, and were machined from the solid. The little-end bearings are bushed, and are splash lubricated by means of an oil hole drilled from the top of the rod. Fully floating gudgeon pins are used with pressed-in end pads to prevent their damaging the cylinder bores. The light alloy pistons are well ribbed internally under the crown and around the gudgeon pin bosses. Four rings are fitted, the lowest one being for oil control.

As mentioned previously, the cylinder head to block joint is simplified by the absence of water passages between the block and head; this

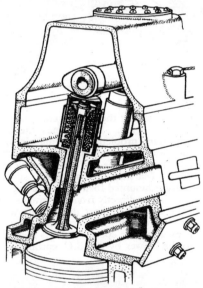

Unlike the arrangement on the standard engine, the overhead valves are inclined in the head and operated by inverted tappets which slide in guides pressed into the cylinder head. The exhaust valves are sodium cooled.

enables the head to be lapped directly on to the block, or a thin steel gasket to be used, and, further to improve sealing qualities, the holes in the gasket are made slightly larger than the cylinder bores. This results in a small groove between the block and head when the components are assembled, which very quickly becomes filled with carbon when the engine is running, and helps to form a perfect seal.

Unlike the production Wolseley engine, where the tappets are attached to the valves, the single overhead camshaft in the record car engine operates the valves by means of inverted tappets which enclose the valve springs and slide in guides pressed into the cylinder head. Sodium-filled exhaust valves of 1.3in diameter are used to assist cooling; the inlet valves are of

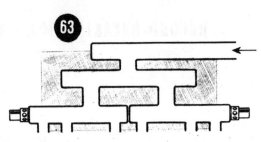

A diagrammatic view of the inlet manifold arrangement used to obtain uniform distribution.

1.38in diameter, and both sets of valves are Stellite-tipped on the tappet face.

The camshaft is driven by two pairs of skew gears and a vertical shaft, as in the Wolseley unit. However, the special silent drive feature used on the standard engine (the lower vertical-shaft gear is split and one half is torsionally loaded against the other) has been eliminated to prevent any possible variation in valve and ignition timing when working under the strenuous conditions imposed during a record run. Again, on the Wolseley unit the distributor is mounted vertically in front of the engine. In this position it would protrude right through the top of the body panels on the record car, and so the ignition is provided by means of a Lucas magneto mounted horizontally behind the engine and driven through the rear of the camshaft. It is fitted with automatic advance mechanism.

Lubrication

Much has been done to ensure that enough oil at the desired temperature (70 deg C) gets where it is wanted. With the supercharged engine the oil consumption is likely to be higher than with a normal unsupercharged unit, as there are extra components that require lubrication, and to cater for this and other demands brought about by high speed operation, provision is made to replenish the sump automatically while the car is in motion. A float chamber is fitted to the left side of the sump and is fed from an auxiliary oil tank. As the sump oil is used, fresh oil automatically flows in and the correct level is maintained. Oil from the

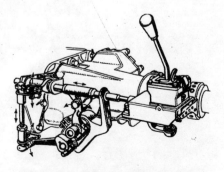

The side levers normally used in conjunction with a steering column gear change mechanism are coupled to an externally mounted remote control mechanism attached to the rear end of the gear box.

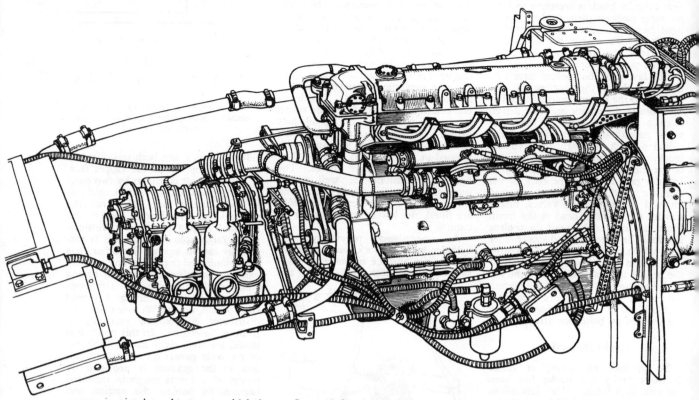

sump is piped to the pump, which is fitted low down on the front of the engine. From the delivery side of the pump it is forced through a full-flow filter, and after passing the filter it flows forward again to the oil cooler, which is placed on top of the water radiator. The cooled oil then travels back through the flexible pipe and into the main oil gallery. A further pipe from the engine supplies oil to the supercharger.

So much for the general construction of the engine. Now comes the all-important problem of getting air and fuel into the cylinders. On this 2-litre power unit this is performed by means of a Marshall (Roots-type) super-charger mounted forward of the engine and driven directly from the crankshaft by means of a short drive shaft with two universal joints; consequently it runs at engine speed. Fuel is metered to the blower by two S.U. carburettors

of 2.375in diameter. The supercharger, then, sucks from the carburettors, thereby eliminating the need for float chamber pressurization of the type necessary when the blower forces air through the carburettors. On the other hand, of course, it means that the supercharger has to pass a mixture of air and fuel and not just air.

From the blower a long pipe conveys the mixture to the manifolds. These are somewhat complicated in design and can best be described as an attempt to achieve the one-time popular political slogan of "fair shares for all." The blower feed pipe terminates in a buffer end with a branch which, set at right-angles to the feed pipe, conveys the mixture to the "first tube" running parallel to the engine. This tube, which also has buffer ends, has two outlet branches, and these in turn feed two more tubes, also parallel to the engine, which have three outlet branches feeding into the cylinder head. In section the unit looks rather like a family tree, where the father has two sons who in turn both have three children. Two blow-off valves are fitted to the outer ends of the second parallel tubes, and these tubes also carry the injectors for the Ki-gass starting equipment.

With the body removed the general layout of the chassis components can be seen. Two large saddle tanks are mounted each side of the chassis in a position where they are well within the wheel-base. The driver sits low down to the right of the propeller-shaft, and, again to reduce the overall height, a special type of steering wheel is used.

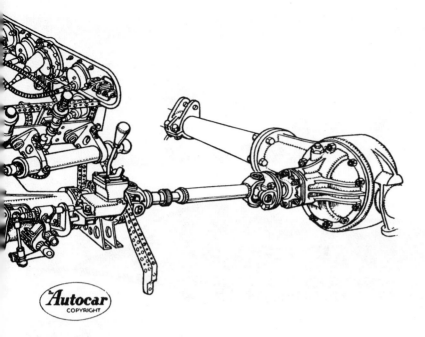

SPECIFICATION

Engine.—6 cylinders, 73.5 × 77.5 mm (1,973 c.c.). Four-bearing crankshaft, single overhead camshaft, operating valves side by side in the head. 31.88 m.p.h. per 1,000 r.p.m. engine speed.

Supercharger.—Marshall (Roots type) shaft driven from crankshaft; set to produce 8-10 lb per sq in.

Clutch.—Borg and Beck, 10in diameter, dry single-plate, centrifugally assisted.

Gear Box.—Four forward speeds: overall ratios, top 2.8 to 1, third 4.05 to 1, second 6.3 to 1, first 9.0 to 1 and reverse 9.0 to 1.

Final Drive.—Straight cut bevel gears, ratio 2.8 to 1.

Suspension.—Front, beam axle with two half-elliptic leaf springs. Friction-type dampers. Rear, underslung Hotchkiss drive with leaf springs and friction-type dampers.

Brakes.—Fitted to rear wheels only, cable operated; 13in diameter, 1⅛ in wide.

Steering.—Bishop Cam steering box, with central swing link and double track rods. Oblong quickly detachable steering wheel.

Wheels and Tyres.—5.25-19in on centre-lock wire wheels.

Ignition.—Lucas magneto.

Fuel System.—Two saddle tanks, 30 gallons total. Fuel supply by means of manifold pressure.

Main Dimensions.—Wheelbase 8ft 3in. Track 4ft (front and rear). Overall length 16ft 5in; width 5ft 3in; height 3ft 6in. Frontal area 9 sq ft.

Weight.—20 cwt approx.

The 2-litre engine is supercharged by a Marshall blower fed by two S.U. carburettors. To keep overall height of the car as low as possible a scuttle mounted radiator header tank is used and the ignition is provided by a Lucas magneto driven from the rear end of the camshaft.

Fuel is supplied to the carburettors by means of two pipe lines from the two saddle tanks, which are mounted well within the wheelbase to reduce to a minimum the effect on weight distribution that is a result of the variation in the amount of fuel carried. The tanks are both pressurized, thereby eliminating the need for a fuel pump when the engine is running. A hand pump is provided to pressurize the system initially, and once the engine is running manifold pressure maintains the flow of fuel.

Now the required fuel tank pressure is only about 4lb per sq in, yet for long-distance records the blower is set to produce 8-10lb per sq in. It is therefore necessary to prevent the tank from becoming too inflated. This is achieved by means of a spring-loaded piston valve which automatically cuts off the air (or, in fact, mixture) supply to the tank when the pre-determined pressure is reached.

Centrifugal Clutch

Power from the engine is transmitted by means of a 10-inch diameter dry single-plate Borg and Beck clutch. It is centrifugally assisted to increase its torque-carrying capacity; this is done by arranging for the centrifugal forces caused by rotation to supplement the spring load on the clutch pressure plate. Consequently, for a given pedal pressure at low speeds, the carrying capacity at maximum torque speed can be considerably more than would be possible without the centrifugal assistance. Alternatively, disregarding pedal pressure, a centrifugally assisted clutch will, for a given diameter of plate, transmit more torque (at speed) than the normal type of clutch. This results in a useful saving in weight. The gear box is a modified Wolseley unit, and for use in this car it is fitted with a remote control gear change mechanism mounted externally on the left side of the box and coupled to the levers normally used for the steering column control.

Owing to the very specialized use for which this car is designed (its purpose is to go very fast in a straight line or to lap a very large-radius circuit), its chassis components are very different from those of a present-day Grand Prix car,

for example. The suspension is very stiff, and only very small spring movements are permitted. The spring deflection from static laden to full bump position at the front is only 1in, and at the rear 2in of movement are permitted.

To reduce the unsprung weight at the front, the brakes are fitted to the rear wheels only. These are mechanically operated and work in drums of 13in diameter and 1⅛in width. Again, because of the particular operating conditions, they are required only to slow the car gradually and not to provide the measure of retardation that is required on a racing car.

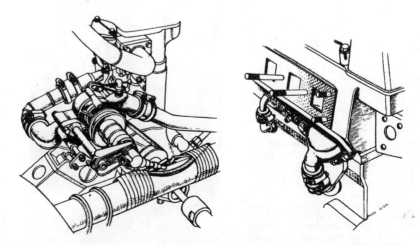

The water pump is belt driven by a pulley on the crankshaft. A spare belt is taped to the cross member in a position where it can be quickly fitted. There are no water passages in the cylinder head joint face ; consequently a transfer pipe (right) conveys the water from the end of the cylinder block to the cylinder head.

GARDNER'S M.G. RECORDS

Supercharged TD-engined Car Achieves Over 202 m.p.h. for the Flying Kilometre at Bonneville

THE CAR: .Goldie Gardner's ·streamlined M.G. about to attack Class E records at Bonneville.

As reported in last week's issue, Goldie Gardner broke five International class records, and set up 16 new records in the American national category, with his streamlined M.G. on the salt flats at Bonneville, Utah.

The poor state of the course was responsible for a near-disaster when the car broadsided on a wet patch, spun completely round and struck a post. The cockpit cover was smashed and Gardner was cut about the face. This incident also resulted in damage to the single-o.h.c., six-cylinder engine which was being used for Class E attempts. A few days later, the Shorrock-supercharged, 1,250 c.c., four-cylinder TD engine was installed and several Class F records, including two International ones, were captured. The flying kilometre (American National Class) was covered at the astonishing speed of 202.14 m.p.h., quite an achievement for a small-capacity, push-rod power-unit.

The 2-litre "six", illustrated in AUTOSPORT, dated 11th July, is purely an experimental unit developed from the existing Wolseley "6-80" engine. Bore and stroke are 73.5 and 77.5 mm. (1,973 c.c.). The cylinder head is of M.G. design, having inclined valves placed in a single row and operated from a skew-gear-driven overhead camshaft via inverted "jam-pot" tappets which totally enclose the double valve springs. Sodium-cooling is used for the exhaust valves.

Separate cylinder head cooling is adopted, coolant passing direct through

THE MAN: Gardner receives first-aid treatment for facial cuts when a marker post shattered the plastic cockpit.

the head passages via a transfer pipe from the block to the rear of the head, and thence back to the header tank by way of a front outlet pipe.

Supercharging is by a Roots-type Marshall instrument running at engine speed and driven direct from the nose of the crankshaft by a short universally-jointed drive shaft. Fuel is drawn from a pair of 2.375 ins. SU carburetters. Supercharger pressure is 8-10 lb. per sq. in.

Transmission is via a centrifugally-assisted Borg and Beck 10 ins. clutch and a Wolseley gearbox, which has the steering-column change-speed mechanism modified to permit the use of a remote-control lever on the end of the box.

THE RECORDS GARDNER TOOK

INTERNATIONAL CLASS E (1,501-2,000 c.c.)

(Standing start)

50 Kiloms.—142.23 m.p.h. (old record, 126.8 m.p.h.).

50 Miles.—147.40 m.p.h. (144.0 m.p.h.).

100 Kiloms.—148.72 m.p.h. (128.1 m.p.h.).

INTERNATIONAL CLASS F (1,101-1,500 c.c.)

(Flying start)

5 Miles.—189.50 m.p.h. (139.2 m.p.h.)
10 Kiloms.—182.84 m.p.h. (138.9 m.p.h.).

American National Records

The following standing start **American National Class E** Records were also taken: 25 kiloms., 133.28 m.p.h; 25 miles, 140.82; 50 kiloms., 143.23; 50 miles, 147.39; 75 kiloms., 146.87; 100 kiloms., 148.72. **Flying start.**—25 kiloms, 155.70; 25 miles, 155.16; 50 kiloms., 155.07; 50 miles, 154.95; 75 kiloms, 154.98. **American National Class F** (flying start).—1 kilom. 202.14; 1 mile, 202.02; 5 kiloms., 200.20; 5 miles, 189.50; 10 kiloms., 182.84.

*　　　*　　　*

The Motor Road Test No. 15/52

Make: M.G. **Type:** Midget Series TD 2-seater

Makers: M.G. Car Co., Ltd., Abingdon-on-Thames, Berks.

Dimensions and Seating

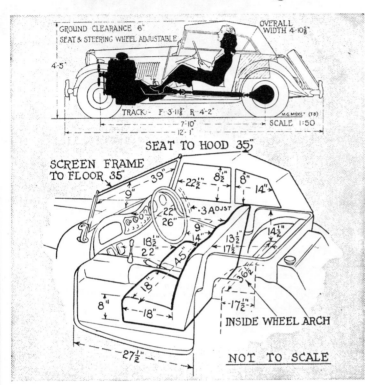

GROUND CLEARANCE 6"
SEAT & STEERING WHEEL ADJUSTABLE
OVERALL WIDTH 4'·10⅜"
4'·5"
TRACK:- F· 3'·11¾" R·4'·2"
M.G. MIDGET (TD)
7'·10"
12'·1"
SCALE 1:50

SEAT TO HOOD 35"
SCREEN FRAME TO FLOOR 35"
39"
9"
22½"
8½"
8"
14"
22"
26"
·3A ADJST
9"
14"
13½"
17½"
14½"
14¼"
18½"
22"
·45"
·36·2"
18"
8"
18"
17½"
27½"
INSIDE WHEEL ARCH
NOT TO SCALE

Test Conditions

Cool, dry weather with moderate cross wind. Smooth tarmac road surface. Car tested with hood and all sidescreens in place.

Test Data

ACCELERATION TIMES on Two Upper Ratios

	Top	3rd
10-30 m.p.h.	9.9 secs.	6.8 secs.
20-40 m.p.h.	10.3 secs.	6.5 secs.
30-50 m.p.h.	12.5 secs.	7.9 secs.
40-60 m.p.h.	15.2 secs.	10.6 secs.
50-70 m.p.h.	20.7 secs	—

ACCELERATION TIMES Through Gear

0-30 m.p.h.	4.5 secs.
0-40 m.p.h.	7.4 secs.
0-50 m.p.h.	12.2 secs
0-60 m.p.h.	18.2 secs.
0-70 m.p.h.	29.5 secs.
Standing Quarter Mile	21.7 secs.

FUEL CONSUMPTION

38.0 m.p.g. at constant 30 m.p.h.
34.0 m.p.g. at constant 40 m.p.h.
27.5 m.p.g. at constant 50 m.p.h.
22.0 m.p.g. at constant 60 m.p.h.
17.5 m.p.g. at constant 70 m.p.h.
Overall consumption for 567 miles, 21¼ gallons
=26.7 m.p.g.

MAXIMUM SPEEDS
Flying Quarter Mile

Mean of four opposite runs	77.2 m.p.h.
Best time equals	78.3 m.p.h.

Speed in Gears

Max. speed in 3rd gear	62 m.p.h.
Max. speed in 2nd gear	41 m.p.h.

WEIGHT

Unladen kerb weight	17½ cwt.
Front/rear weight distribution	50/50
Weight laden as tested	21 cwt.

INSTRUMENTS

Speedometer at 30 m.p.h.	6% slow
Speedometer at 60 m.p.h.	3% slow
Distance recorder	1% fast

HILL CLIMBING (at steady speeds)

Max. top gear speed on 1 in 20	65 m.p.h.
Max. top gear speed on 1 in 15	58 m.p.h.
Max. top gear speed on 1 in 10	32 m.p.h.
Max. gradient on top gear	1 in 10 (Tapley 225 lb./ton)
Max. gradient on 3rd gear	1 in 7.1 (Tapley 310 lb./ton)
Max. gradient on 2nd gear	1 in 5 (Tapley 440 lb./ton)

BRAKES at 30 m.p.h.

0.99 g retardation	(=30½ ft. stopping distance)	with 100 lb. pedal pressure
0.70 g retardation	(=43 ft. stopping distance)	with 75 lb. pedal pressure
0.43 g retardation	(=70 ft. stopping distance)	with 50 lb. pedal pressure
0.14 g retardation	(=215 ft. stopping distance)	with 25 lb. pedal pressure

In Brief

Price £530 plus purchase tax £295 18s. 11d. equals £825 18s. 11d.

Capacity	1,250 c.c.
Unladen kerb weight	17½ cwt.
Fuel consumption	26.7 m.p.g.
Maximum speed	77.2 m.p.h.
Maximum speed on 1 in 20 gradient	65 m.p.h.
Maximum top gear gradient	1 in 10

Acceleration

10-30 m.p.h. in top	9.9 secs.
0-50 m.p.h. through gears	12.2 secs.

Gearing 14.4 m.p.h. in top at 1000 r.p.m. 61 m.p.h. at 2500 ft. per min. piston speed.

Specification

Engine

Cylinders	4
Bore	66.5 mm.
Stroke	90 mm
Cubic capacity	1,250 c.c.
Piston area	21.6 sq. in.
Valves	Pushrod o.h.v.
Compression ratio	7.25/1 (Optional 8.6/1 or 9.3/1 ratios available to suit special fuels)
Max. power	54.4 b.h.p.
at	5,200 r.p.m.
Piston speed at max. b.h.p.	3,070 ft. per min.
Carburetter	2 inclined S.U.
Ignition	12-volt coil
Sparking plugs	14 mm. Champion L10S
Fuel pump	S.U. electrical
Oil filter	Purolator by-pass

Transmission

Clutch	8-in. s.d.p.
Top gear (s/m)	5.125 (Optional at extra cost, 4.875 or 4.55)
3rd gear (s/m)	7 098
2nd gear (s/m)	10.61
1st gear	17.94
Propeller shaft	Hardy Spicer open
Final drive	8/41 Hypoid bevel

Chassis

Brakes	Lockheed hydraulic (2 l.s. front
Brake drum diameter	9 ins.
Friction lining area	99.5 sq. ins.
Suspension: Front	Coil and wishbone I.F.S.
Rear	Semi-elliptic
Shock absorbers	Girling piston-type
Tyres	Dunlop 5.50-15

Steering

Steering gear	Rack and pinion
Turning circle	31¼ ft.
Turns of steering wheel, lock to lock	2²/₃

Performance factors (at laden weight as tested)

Piston area sq. in. per ton	20.6
Brake lining area, sq. in. per ton	95
Specific displacement, litres per ton mile	2,480

Fully described in "The Motor," January 18, 1950

Maintenance

Fuel tank: 12½ gallons (Warning light indicates last 2¼ gallons). **Sump:** 10½ pints, S.A.E. 30. **Gear box:** 1¼ pints, S.A.E. 90 gear oil. **Rear axle:** 2¼ pints S.A.E. 90 hypoid oil. **Steering gear:** S.A.E. 90 gear oil **Radiator:** 14 pints (2 drain taps). **Chassis lubrication:** by grease gun every 500 miles to 6 points. Every 1000 miles to 3 points. Every 3000 miles to 1 point. Every 6000 miles to 1 point. **Ignition timing:** T.D.C. static. **Spark plug gap:** 0.020-0.022 in. **Contact breaker gap:** 0.010-0.012 in. **Valve timing:** I.O., 11° b.t.d.c.; I.C., 57° a.b.d.c.; E.O., 52° b.b.d.c.; E.C., 24° a.t.d.c. **Tappet clearances (cold):** Inlet and Exhaust, 0.020 in. **Front wheel toe-in:** nil **Camber angle:** 1° positive (± 1°). **Castor angle:** 2 (± ½°). **Tyre pressures:** Front 18 lb., Rear 18-22 lb. (See text) **Brake fluid:** Lockheed orange. **Battery:** 12 volt, 51 amp. hr **Lamp bulbs:** 12 volt. Headlamps 42/36 watt, Sidelamps and number plate lamp 6 watt, stop/tail lamps 18/6 watt. (Lamps are of the double dipping type with block lenses).   Ref. B/13/52.

The M.G. MIDGET Series TD

A Popular Sporting Two-seater of Sturdy Build

OF one thing the builder of a popular-priced sports car can be sure. that his products will be driven very hard indeed by the majority of their purchasers. Few models can have withstood such treatment more successfully than has the TD series M.G. Midget. which can now claim to be fully proven by 2½ years of

FULL PROTECTION against bad weather is available, in the form of an easily erected hood and four transparent side-screens.

READY TO HAND in the cockpit are the fly-off racing handbrake and the short remote-control gear lever. Individual cushions and an adjustable single-piece shaped backrest form the unusual but comfortable seats.

large-scale production, so it was with great interest that we recently tested such a car in order to refresh our memories of miles covered in an early production example.

For a long while. the view was widely held that the small sporting car was a peculiarly British folly, this type of vehicle being quite unsuited to use elsewhere in the world. Such views have always been to some extent false but it has nevertheless been left to the "TD" really to prove that the right sort of sports car can in fact be one of this country's best-selling export products. Offering all the traditional characteristics of responsive steering. willing cornering, and an engine-gearbox unit which responds to skilled handling, this model also offers the sturdiness and excellence of design which allows it to withstand hard driving in mountainous country or over unmade tracks just as readily as it copes with England's congested but tolerably well-surfaced roads. Perhaps the most important aspect of the car's character showed up as it was driven along a winding gravel track which was criss-crossed with rain-water gullies and sprinkled with huge water-filled potholes: although more firmly sprung than the average touring car, the Midget tackled such going at a brisk pace with as little bumping or weaving as would any all-steel saloon.

Testing the Midget in England, the major part of our driving was of course over much smoother surfaces. but it remains true that this is a very comfortably sprung sports model. with springs firm enough to allow four individual bumps to be felt as the car is driven diagonally off a raised kerb, but nevertheless giving a level ride unbroken by major shocks. In comparison with older types of sports car, this suspension is definitely soft, and there is an appreciable amount of roll to be observed during fast cornering, but we did not find any reason to object to this suspension flexibility—which. if desired, can be restrained to suit personal tastes by the fitting of "optional extra" friction shock absorbers to supplement the usual hydraulic damping.

Light and Sensitive Steering

Rack and pinion steering gear has a reputation for sensitivity. and the gear fitted to this model is no exception to the rule. Geared quite moderately at just over 2½ turns from extreme to extreme of its very good lock, the steering is very light and free from lost motion. On smooth roads, a small amount of static friction can be felt, so that the gentle self-centring action is inoperative for small deflections from a straight course: rough surfaces, on the other hand, produce quite appreciable shake of the steering wheel, but without impairing control. One point concerning which we found ourselves in disagreement with the official recommendations was tyre pressures—the suggested equal front. and rear pressures of 18 lb. tending to give steering sensitivity so great as to amount to "oversteer," whereas a 3 lb. increase in the rear tyre pressures served to stabilize the car without making it in the slightest degree unresponsive to the helm.

The independently sprung box-section chassis which gives the "TD" roadworthi-

CONSPICUOUS in this view are the spare wheel and 12½-gallon external fuel tank. Extras available to order are a mounting for a second spare wheel, and a luggage grid to supplement luggage space available inside the bodywork.

TRADITIONAL in appearance, the TD-series Midget is a responsive sporting two-seater of proven sturdiness.

ness far superior to that of its predecessors was entirely new in 1950, but the power unit has a rather longer pedigree. In effect, this 1,250 c.c. unit of 11 h.p. rating is the short-stroke successor to the 1,292 c.c., 10 h.p. unit introduced in 1936, when pushrods replaced an overhead camshaft for the actuation of overhead valves. Neat rather than spectacular in appearance, with its four-branch exhaust manifold and twin semi-downdraught carburetters on the offside, this engine has proved capable of withstanding an astonishing amount of tuning when used for racing.

Improved Acceleration

Measured with an ignition setting which produced considerable but certainly not intolerable amounts of low-speed pinking on "Pool" petrol, the acceleration figures recorded upon our data page are quite substantially faster than those timed 2½ years ago on a nominally similar car. Deceived perhaps by casual impressions, formed before we discovered that (on the test car at least) a pessimistic speedometer had replaced the incurably optimistic units of past times, we had not realised quite what rapid acceleration was available until the stop-watches were brought into action. In particular, there was an aural impression that below 35 m.p.h. in top gear the engine scarcely got into its stride, whereas the timed tests revealed notable torque right down to less than 1,000 r.p.m.

Quoted as delivering its maximum power at over 5,000 r.p.m., the engine is manifestly intended to be run fast: a tachometer reading to 6,000 r.p.m. directly faces the driver, and the large dial does not carry any red mark to indicate a recommended limit within this range. It is perfectly possible to potter through towns or down country lanes in top gear, with only a slight irregularity of engine running evident, and the engine's tick-over is both smooth and certain. The car is, however, geared to be able to attain its peak engine r.p.m. in top gear, and gives its best performance when full use is made of the four-speed gearbox. There is a considerable amount of mechanical noise from the valvegear when the car is driven fast, but never any loss of oil pressure, increase in oil consumption or other indication that the engine objects to sustained operation at high speeds.

The actual timed maximum speed of 77.2 m.p.h., as the mean of runs in opposite directions over the ¼ mile, may appear to some people to be modest in relation to a power output of 54 b.h.p. It must be said, however, that speeds within this maximum suffice for many people's requirements, and that the unstreamlined kind of two-seater bodywork which limits maximum speed does provide for very good engine accessibility, modest repair costs in

the event of minor accidents and excellent cooling of the brakes, as well as having appearances which please many people: streamlining could provide a higher top speed, but in so doing it would demand the use of a higher top gear ratio with which good acceleration would be much more dependent upon use of the gearbox.

A significant contribution towards faster through-the-gears acceleration quite evidently comes from an increase in clutch plate diameter which was standardized about a year ago. Without being fierce, the clutch now permits racing-style starts or gear changes to be made usefully when desired, never showing the slightest tendency to slip. On the other hand, it seems probable that the extra spinning weight of the modified clutch must be blamed for some loss of apparent effectiveness of the synchro-mesh mechanism, it now being rather easier than formerly to produce noise by unduly hustling an ordinary upward gear-change. The remote gear control works excellently, but on the test car the spring-resisting sideways motion of the gear-lever towards the "reverse" position was rather on the light side.

Good Stopping Power

Brakes have a great deal of work to do on a sports car, and those on the "TD" seemed to be well up to their job. The stopping power built up progressively with increasing pedal pressure until all wheels locked together, and although two-leading-shoe brakes inherently have less power during reversing this characteristic was not unduly pronounced. The fly-off handbrake, set horizontally between the seats, is comfortable to use and well able to lock the rear wheels.

The M.G. body is of traditional style, but quite usefully wider than on earlier models, and by sports car standards quite reasonably easy to enter. An unusual form of seat adjustment is provided, two separate seat cushions adjusting individually fore-and-aft, and a single backrest extending right across the car having adjustable rake: within limits, there is unusually good scope

for obtaining an ideal driving position, a telescopic steering column being an additional help to this end, but the single-piece backrest limits the scope for suiting both a driver and a passenger.

Driving vision from a rather low seating position is generally good, whether the hood be erect or folded, with the exception of one point: mounted on the scuttle, to give proper vision rearwards even if the windscreen is folded flat, the metal-framed driving mirror does conceal a nearside front wing which otherwise would just be visible over the flat bonnet top. The use of four transparent sidescreens means that there are no bad blind spots even when the car is completely closed.

The hood is quite easy to erect or fold in changeable weather, and the rear tonneau cover is also very easy to fit: this latter is neatly tensioned with elastic, but both it and the hood are made in a coarse material which is perhaps strong but certainly lacks good looks. A locker is provided for the sidescreens, but two annoyances were the need to remove the rear sidescreens before fitting or removing the tonneau cover, and a slight tendency for exhaust fumes to be drawn forward into the car if the hood was lowered and all four sidescreens left in position.

External headlamps are nowadays a rarity, and whilst easily adjusted they can also easily be put out of line by man-handling in a garage. On the test car, they were set to give a very low beam indeed, but ideally adjusted they should give a good driving light, usefully high mountings helping to eliminate shadows on undulating road. At night, we found the speedometer and tachometer illumination rather too bright, although the oil pressure gauge and ammeter had much gentler lighting: we also found the switchgear slightly "fiddling" for gloved hands, although an impending change from hand to foot controlled headlamp dipping will eliminate one switch on the facia panel. Quite why the facia carries no gauge indicating the level in the huge fuel tank, but only a low-level warning lamp, we are unable to explain.

After a week during which many members of our staff used the M.G. for very varied runs, we parted with it quite sadly. Relatively inexpensive, and an entirely practical, quiet vehicle for everyday business or shopping errands, it also roars away in very entertainingly brisk fashion whenever the mood or the need for fast travel occurs.

STRAIGHTFORWARD in design, the twin-carburetter engine has in-line overhead valves operated by pushrods. An oil-bath air cleaner on the carburetter intake typifies the suitability of the model for export markets.

The TD above is styled in more smoothly flowing lines than its predecessor, the TC, much to the sorrow of the old guard.

For competition or safe, economical transportation, John Bull's version of the Model A has no peer in the sports car field.

1952 TD On Trial

Text and Photos by

M. B. CARROLL, JR.

SPEED AGE FEATURE WRITER

SPEED AGE—America's FIRST Motor Racing Magazine

WEBSTER defines "ubiquitous" as "existing everywhere" but I say that the word really means "MG". There never has been a race, rally, or concourse that didn't see hundreds of these endearing little carts in all stages of tune and ornamentation.

Rugged enough to withstand all but the most serious attempts to blow them up, economical to buy ($2,115) and operate, and making up in manueverability what it lacks in performance, John Bull's version of the Model A has been responsible for many an American dollar's trans-atlantic journey—eastward, that is.

The saucy installation of the spare, a crowning styling touch by the designer.

MGs flow from the Abington-on-the-Thames Nuffield factory in a never ending, multi-colored stream and the demand for new models is exceeded only by that for used ones.

The urge to own an MG isn't based on performance, as several cars in its class will outperform it; there are roomier, more comfortable sports cars available but none capture the spirit of the thing as does the MG.

Here, for a price roughly equivalent to that of a Ford, is transportation and the opportunity to be grouped by the populace as a whole in that category of the most heroic of 'hero drivers.' Here is the answer for couples whose budget has restricted them to the same type car as the man next door. Doors, that would be slammed in the face of anyone driving a Chevy, swing wide to the MG owner. A rather pleasant form of snobbery, combined with easy parking, and all for $2115? Speed up the production line,

Simplicity itself marks the radiator, flanked by good and honest fenders.

The rugged front suspension consists of A-frames and coil springs. The steering linkage is ahead of the kingpins. Rear of this car uses semi-elliptic springs.

Reggie, we've got something here!

Inspected with a critical eye, the appearance is similar to many American roadsters of the early '30s—it has fenders, good honest fenders that don't play at being a jet plane—the headlights sit out in the open between the fenders and the bonnet (hood to you, Bud) and the spare tire reclines at a sassy angle in full view at the rear.

The spare tire was the final touch of genius applied by the styling department —my introduction to sports cars was the spare tire of a TD disappearing in the distance. There's nothing more irritating than to command three times the power, purchased at half again the price, and then have one of these spare tires thumb its nose at you as it disappears around a turn.

It's a matter of record that when I could stand it no longer I bought one, drove it home, and in the privacy of the garage proceeded to kick that tire black and blue. Then I went out on the highway and blew off everything American that I could goad into chasing me—it was so much fun that I became a real sports car bug and now the only people who speak to me are other sports car bugs.

But this is a test report, not a biography. So let's lift the hood and see what supplies the 'urge.' There are four cylinders and they'll push out 54 horses at 5200 RPM. With a bore and stroke of 2.62 x 3.54 inches, piston speeds are quite high—particularly when compared with the more modern square or oversquare engines such as the Porsche. The generally accepted 2,500 feet per minute piston speed for cruising is reached at slightly over 4000 RPM, giving a road speed of 61 MPH. Beyond this the car tends to get too noisy for my comfort.

Valves are pushrod operated overhead and the chances are that the painted sheet metal top and side covers have been replaced with the polished aluminum ones made in this country. The manufacture of MG accessories is big business and production of valve covers, side plates, and plastic wind-wings is big enough to justify using the most modern tooling methods.

Carburetion is supplied, as on the majority of English cars, by the S.U. side-draft units. For some unknown reason, there is but one air cleaner, perched atop a pipe which branches to each carburetor. This abomination is generally removed as soon as the new owner can purchase a pair of chrome-plated Hellings cleaners. The difference in the amount of air received at the carburetors is great enough to make re-adjustment mandatory.

Differing from some of its hotter (literally) brethren, the MG possesses a thoroughly adequate cooling system. I never have heard of an MG that overheated. Late models are fitted with a water temperature gauge—favored accessory for the earlier models is the old, small diameter Moto-Meter but they are hard to find.

The chassis layout is conventional with an independent front end (coil springs) and a solid rear axle with semi-elliptic springs. The secrets of this wagon's road-holding aren't secrets at all—they're just good basic design, practically even weight distribution fore and aft, husky shock absorbers combined with soft enough springs to let it hold on the bumpy as well as the smooth courses, low center of gravity, 94 inch wheelbase, and light, fast rack and pinion steering. Anent the latter, (technical inspectors please note) the grease retaining ball in the fitting that lubricates the rack has displayed an occasional tendency to drop between the rack and the pinion. This happened to my good friend Irv Roth not so long ago and he found himself with a car suitable for a course 75 feet in diameter—no more. no less. Change to an American fitting if you already own a TD and save some embarrassment and possibly your life.

New instruments, with variable intensity lighting, are easy to read. Later models also have water temperature gauge. The large dial, seen through the steering wheel, is the PerfOmeter. The steering wheel has an in-and-out adjustment. Note hand grip at the extreme left.

The aluminum valve cover and side plate are generally added by MG owners. However the Mallory ignition and Hellings air cleaners would place this car in the modified class but are typical of those done by the many MG enthusiasts.

As a competition car, the MG has no peer. I don't mean to infer that there aren't hotter cars, for there are many, but have you ever seen a stock MG race? Better yet, have you ever raced one? My first was a stock MG event and there's nothing to equal the thrill that comes from being in the middle of a pack of identical automobiles and knowing that you've nothing but tuning and driving skill to get you out front. Some of the best duels ever seen have been in the stock races—those of Cunningham and Plaisted, Bird and Said, and Newcombe and Mauren at Allentown and Thompson stand out in my mind and there are others —the Allards, Cunninghams, and Ferraris may turn in higher speeds but they don't have any more fun.

If you want to race your MG, leave it strictly stock. Modify and you'll be running against the OSCA, the Porsche, and other equipment that will leave you flat. All the effort in the world won't make your true sports car into something that can race on equal terms with cars designed specifically for competition.

Knowing I'd get a properly tuned car for performance tests from Al Hanusocky of Havell Motors, I called him and was rewarded when he volunteered his own MG. Although not strictly stock—having Hellings air cleaners and Mallory ignition —the modifications are typical of those done by many enthusiasts and the performance can therefore be judged as representative of the average MG you are likely to encounter on the road.

Using my newly acquired PerfoMeter to determine the optimum shifting points, I clocked 0 to 60 MPH in 12.3 seconds, the standing quarter mile in 20 seconds flat, and showed a two-way average of 84.7 MPH on a better than two mile straight. This was done with the windscreen lowered and the tonneau cover over the passenger's seat.

This was the first I'd driven an MG in several months and, as always, I was amazed at the handling ease—two and three quarter turns will take the wheel from lock to lock (exactly twice as fast as my '49 Lincoln), the pedals are close enough together that it's easy for even my small feet to hit the brake, gas, and clutch simultaneously as in hard cornering. The brakes are all anyone could ask —exactly 141 feet to a dead stop from 60 MPH—short of using an anchor: I don't see how that could be improved upon for it represents a stopping force equal to about .8G, generally referred to as 80% braking efficiency, and is close to the coefficient of friction of rubber on smooth asphalt. Beyond that point you slide, the coefficient of friction decreases, and your stopping distances increases.

Brake fade is practically non-existent although I did notice a slight trace after the aforementioned stock MG race—20 laps and 80 severe applications on a hot day.

Although I can recall an occasion when we jammed four into an MG, the factory's designation of "two-seater" is correct. The emergency brake and the short

gearshift lever effectively divide the seat. I have, however, seen several of these cars rigged up with an extra windscreen to provide protection for children riding in the luggage locker behind the seat. Judging by what I've been able to cram into that locker I'll take an oath that it stretches.

It will hold three small suitcases and an incredible amount of odds and ends stuffed into the nooks and crannies. The cubby locker (that's the dash compartment, Son) is larger than those on most of the cars produced here.

Upholstery is genuine leather and, in the usual forward and back slide, there is provision for changing the angle of the back of the seat. The wheel, as on the Jaguar, has an in-and-out adjustment.

The usual, complete tool kit is furnished along with an instruction book that's a marvel of completeness and clarity. The top material may be extremely durable but it's a masterpiece of ugliness, nonetheless. The side curtains, as on any sports car, provide token protection against the rain. While the factory provides no heater, the MG heater made in this country is of such capacity that it is rarely used to its full capabilities. Buy one and you'll never have a frigid Midget.

With one exception, I think the MG is one of the safest cars on the road today. Contrary to the current American practice, its roadability exceeds its performance potential. Its sturdiness has turned many a potentially dangerous roadracing accident into a mere incident. Most important of all, these cars are very dear to the hearts of their owners and a loving owner will go far out of his way to avoid an accident.

The exception I mentioned is the unfortunate placing of the windshield wiper motor and its switch in line with the passenger's forehead. With such powerful brakes, a panic stop could well be fatal to an unsuspecting companion.

Last year the factory announced the Mark II, a hotted up version of the standard job. Eight shocks, instead of the usual four, improved cornering, while larger carburetors, oversize valves, heavier valve springs and two fuel pumps added some 10 HP. The factory then proceeded to nullify these advantages by fitting a higher rear end ratio (4.875 instead of the standard 5.125), resulting in less acceleration than the standard model albeit producing a few more miles per hour at the top of the scale. I was not impressed except with the one owned by a friend who managed to get delivery prior to the time he actually turned his trade-in, a standard job, over to the dealer. It was only a few hours work to swap the rear ends and the result was wonderful to behold. I often wonder, though, about the poor chap who bought the trade-in.

CONTINUED ON PAGE 89

ROAD and TRACK ROAD TEST No. F-2-53

MG TD and MG TDC (Mark II)

SPECIFICATIONS

	TD	TDC
Wheelbase	94.0 in.	94.0 in.
Tread—front	47.4 in.	47.4 in.
—rear	50.0 in.	50.0 in.
Tire size	5.50 x 15	5.50 x 15
Curb weight (Lbs)	2005	2015
—front	985	990
—rear	1020	1025
Cylinders	4, in line	
Valve system	ohv, pushrod	
Bore & stroke	66.5 x 90 mm	
	2.62 x 3.54 in.	
Displacement	1250 cc	
	76.3 cu in.	
Horsepower	54	60
At rpm	5200	5500
Compression ratio	7.25	8.10
Gear ratios—4th	5.125	4.875
3rd	7.098	6.750
2nd	10.61	10.10
1st	17.94	17.08
Mph Per 1000 rpm	14.4	15.2
List price	$2157	$2380

MG Model TD Performance Data

TAPLEY READINGS

Pulling Power	Gear	mph
423 lbs per ton	1st	22
372 lbs per ton	2nd	31
273 lbs per ton	3rd	36
195 lbs per ton	4th	36

Deceleration Rate (Coasting)

14 lbs per ton at	10 mph
36 lbs per ton at	30 mph
103 lbs per ton at	60 mph

ACCELERATION

0-30 mph	5.2 secs.
0-40 mph	8.8 secs.
0-50 mph	13.8 secs.
0-60 mph	19.4 secs.
0-70 mph	31.8 secs.
Standing ¼ mile	21.3 secs.

SHIFTING POINTS

From	At
1st gear	24 mph
2nd gear	40 mph
3rd gear	60 mph

SPEEDOMETER ERROR

Speedometer	Actual
20 mph	20.0
30 mph	26.7
40 mph	35.7
50 mph	44.1
60 mph	53.2
70 mph	62.0
80 mph	71.4

PERFORMANCE

Test conditions: 30 ft. below sea level; temp. 50°F; clear night, light breeze; driver, passenger, equipment wt. 440 lbs.

Flying ¼ mile	78.9 mph
Fastest one way	79.6 mph

FUEL CONSUMPTION

Actual testing and 50/70 mph highway cruising

(178 miles)	24.3 mpg
City	20/22 mpg

A COMPARISON OF THE STOCK MODEL TD AND THE MARK II

Scattered amidst *Road and Track*'s daily correspondence has been a constant demand for a 1953 MG Road Test (last test, *Road and Track*, April 1951), but in planning the venture the staff felt that not only should the MG TD be thoroughly scrutinized, but the MG TDC (official title of the super-tuned Mark II) as well. The decision to compare both models was finalized due to the volume of mail from readers who were interested in a little more performance than is offered by the MG TD, and who expressed a curiosity about Mark II performance.

For those who may not be familiar with the differences between the model TD and the model TDC, the latter offers certain modifications which include:

1. Higher compression ratio.
2. Larger carburetors.
3. Larger valves.
4. Heavier valve springs.
5. Twin electric fuel pumps.
6. A "faster" rear axle ratio.
7. An additional set of shock absorbers.

Some difficulty was experienced in obtaining a TD and TDC of relatively equal mileage and overall condition so that a fair comparison could be made. Two cars meeting all requirements were those owned by Bill Corey and Ralph Stewart, both of Peter Satori's Pasadena showrooms. It should be mentioned that among the roadsters kindly offered for testing were the TDC's of Ken Miles (MG Factory Service Representative); Ralph Pool (*Hop Up* Magazine Staff Photographer); and a TD belonging to the West Coast MG Distributors, Gough Industries.

Both owners did their own tune up work; both cars were relatively new (4,000/6,000 miles). Corey's car was as delivered except for the addition of 1½ inch lowering blocks (on the rear springs) and dual mufflers. Stewart's car was tested with an airscoop on the right hand hood-side adjacent to the carburetors. The TD dual mufflers had no noticeable effect on performance, and the air scoop on the TDC was installed to maintain peak performance in hot weather. Since the tests were run on a cool night, performance figures are as stock.

Performance . . .

Both cars made their timed top speeds with the side curtains in place and the tops erected. Since there was only a light wind at the time, the averages were but little different from fastest one way runs. One timed run on the TDC was made with the top down and the windshield folded flat (but without benefit of a full length tonneau cover). The top speed was exactly the same as before.

Normally the TDC can be expected to have 5 extra mph over the stock TD on a timed maximum speed check. In this case Corey's TD had been given a valve grind after the breaking-in period (as recommended in the factory manual), while Stewart's TDC had not—which may account for the difference of only 2.3 to 3.3 mph.

A study of the engine torque curves, gear ratios and acceleration characteristics of the two cars brings out some interesting points. The TDC axle ratio reduces the acceleration potential by almost 5% in comparison to the stock TD axle ratio. This loss is not offset by the increased torque of the TDC engine until its revolutions reach approximately 3500. At engine speeds above this rate, the TDC torque advantage over the TD is more than 5%. In fact at 5000 rpm the TDC has

Long and loud has been the controversy. Which is the better car . . . MG TD or Mk II?

MG Model TDC (Mark II) Performance Data

TAPLEY READINGS

Pulling Power	Gear	mph
455 lbs per ton	1st	26
362 lbs per ton	2nd	39
243 lbs per ton	3rd	41
165 lbs per ton	4th	39

Deceleration Rate (Coasting)
10 lbs per ton at........10 mph
30 lbs per ton at........30 mph
103 lbs per ton at........10 mph

ACCELERATION

0-30 mph .... 5.2 secs.
0-40 mph .... 7.5 secs.
0-50 mph .... 11.1 secs.
0-60 mph .... 16.5 secs.
0-70 mph .... 24.4 secs.
Standing ¼ mile ....20.85 secs.

SHIFTING POINTS

From	At
1st gear	28 mph
2nd gear	43 mph
3rd gear	66 mph

SPEEDOMETER ERROR

Speedometer	Actual
20 mph	19.2
30 mph	27.7
40 mph	36.5
50 mph	45.9
60 mph	55.5
70 mph	64.2
80 mph	73.2

PERFORMANCE

Test conditions: 30 ft. below sea level; temp. 50°F; clear night, light breeze; driver, passenger, equipment wt. 440 lbs.
Flying ¼ mile........81.25 mph
Fastest one way........82.9 mph

FUEL CONSUMPTION

Actual testing and 50/70 mph highway cruising
(184 miles) ....21.9 mpg
City .... 16/19 mpg
Country .... 20/23 mpg

an 8.5% advantage which increases to 13% at 5500 rpm.

The result is that in any gear the stock TD is livelier than the TC, so long as the engine speed remains under 3500 rpm. This characteristic shows up on the acceleration comparison curves in first gear only. Note how the TDC lags behind the stock TD initially but catches the TD at about 25 mph, and then goes way out in front as successive gears are engaged. If we plotted acceleration in each gear, starting at, say, 1000 rpm in each case, the low end performance disadvantage of the TDC would show up more prominently.

In any event, the performance tables and curves show not only the comparison between the two MG models, but also point up the fact that a TD is "quicker" than many American cars. The TDC will hold its own on get-away with any but the most powerful models.

Handling Characteristics . . .

Judgment of ride, steering, and handling qualities is not an exact science, but the MG in either model comes awfully close to being the best (and safest) consolidation of these qualities that can be bought.

By sports car standards, the MG rides very well. Rough roads at low speeds do not give the slow motion characteristic of most family cars—in fact, under these conditions some people would say the bumps were very noticeable. On the other hand, the ride is certainly flat and free from pitch or kick. At high speeds the driver and passenger are very comfortable and the car takes rough surfaces, dips, and "thank-you-ma'ms" in a safe and exemplary manner.

The rack and pinion steering is almost ideal, and only falls short of being perfect because of occasional kick-back over certain types of road surfaces. This "feel of the road" is not objectionable, or tiring, but it is there at times.

The actual steering ratio is an excellent compromise between parking requirements and safe handling. Two and two-thirds turns of the wheel take you from a full left to a full right turn, and whether in city traffic, or on winding mountain roads, the driving of this car is sheer pleasure.

Owners will notice that the handbook furnished with the car recommends 18 psi tire pressures all around. One must assume that this idea is directed toward the well-known

American predilection for a soft ride. Actually 18 psi seems far too low for taking best advantage of the MG's maneuverability. Both cars tested at this inflation pressure exhibited the same characteristic while cornering— a tendency for the rear end to become "mushy", and as you went faster the rear end would begin to "walk" outward to such an extent that "back-rudder" had to be used to hold the curve. This condition is, of course, oversteer, and interesting enough, increasing tire pressure to 24-26 psi made a complete change in handling. At 26-28 psi tire howl is very difficult to produce, and 30 psi seemed optimum for best handling with a small but definite amount of desirable understeer.

While the cars do oversteer in a turn with recommended pressures, it must also be recorded that the ride is more comfortable (at 18 psi), and there is no directional instability or steering problem of any kind when cruising in the seventies on straight stretches of highway. For those owners who prefer to run on soft tires, and do not like oversteer, it is possible to install the anti-roll bar used as standard equipment on the

(Continued on next page)

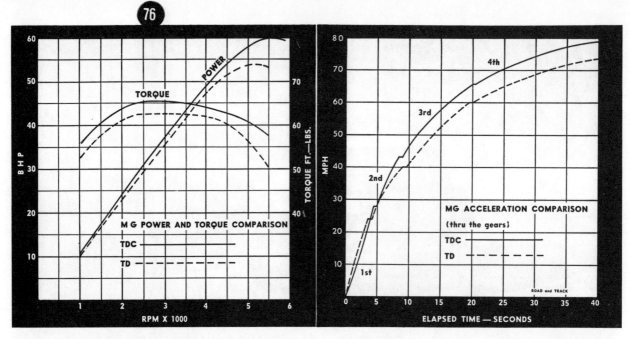

The torque and horsepower of the TDC show substantial improvement over the TD. Torque increase of TDC is a notable achievement in view of better provisions for breathing — normally some loss in torque is expected in order to get higher peak horsepower.

Horizontal jogs in curves indicate gear changes which require approximately one-half second for each shift. Definite superiority of the Mark II when using the gears to best advantage is apparent in this comparison—which also shows both cars equal up to 30 mph.

MG 1¼ litre Series Y sedan. This bar counteracts and reduces the roll angle, produces understeer, and will help to keep the inside rear wheel on the ground for more rapid acceleration out of corners—a desirable condition if you are "going in" for competitions.

The supplementary shock absorbers supplied with the model TDC are adjustable to four positions from "off" to "very firm". Stewart's car's shock absorbers were set at "¾" producing a less comfortable ride than the stock TD model. It was noticeable that with the above setting there was less roll in corners than on the TD and the car felt more secure at high speed .

Special Features . . .

Both the TD and TDC offer the owner excellent value. The leather in MG seats has always been top quality and the seating position is comfortable, providing plenty of elbow room for the passenger and driver. Foot room for the passenger is ample, but the driver's left foot must be held in one of two positions: on the clutch (not recommended), or pulled back and crooked to the side. This may prove disconcerting to the sports car initiate, but the old hand is used to it. The top folds away in a one-man operation and a neat fitting tonneau cover is provided. The side curtains fit well, making the occupants comfortable and snug in all but really severe weather. Some wind turbulence around the windshield is noticed with the top folded back, but whether this is any greater than the average convertible with its windows rolled down is a question for debate. Electric windshield wipers are a boon to those annoyed by the slowing down of the vacuum type when the car is accelerating, and the horn button is on the dash at finger-tip length from the steering wheel. In the past year and a half a number of improvements have been made such as an oil pickup mounted in the center of the sump (previous MG's had a tendency for the oil to pile up on the side of the sump when making a fast left hand bend). The instruments (tachometer and speedometer) have been changed for better visibility, a water temperature gauge has been

The rugged MG TD chassis' box section, side-rails are larger than those of many American cars. The tubular cowl support, used for stiffening the chassis, is an integral part of the frame.

added, and all panel lights are dimmable by rheostat. Other recent changes: a floor dimmer switch; a redesigned water pump seal; a new head with revised ports and longer reach (NA-8) spark plugs; a new rocker arm assembly; new tappets, with special surface treatment; an 8 inch clutch (formerly 7¼ inch); a larger sump; and a new, more accessible oil filter. A 4.55:1 rear axle ratio is an optional extra for the TDC. Along with American specialty houses, MG offers as factory optional equipment: badge bars, driving lights, luggage racks and a glove compartment radio.

Conclusions . . .

In deciding which of the two models to buy, readers should realize that the extra equipment of the TDC (larger carburetors,

extra shock absorbers, higher compression ratio, "faster" rear axle ratio, twin fuel pumps, etc.) cannot be purchased for the same amount of money as the difference in the price of the two cars when new. However, many readers may not care about the greater acceleration available. Conversely, many MG fans will be grateful for the extra equipment—either because they want peak performance or they intend to modify their cars still further.

Remember, the MG is a genuine sports car, with a gearbox designed to be used. If you want maximum performance the TDC will give it, and stand up under extremely hard usage. If you want better tractability, less gear shifting, and somewhat smoother running—better buy the stock TD model. •

The Editor and wife were happy with MG's durability and economy.

35,000 MG MILES

In its 1951 Road Test. *Road and Track* described the MG: "as friendly as a tail-wagging dog". Someone else pointed out: "MG is the only car in the world that sells *personality*". But beyond its winning ways, the MG proved, to me at least, rugged and serviceable. Mine was driven hard, but close attention was paid to proper servicing.

In Southern California, there is an old saw about the used car salesman who confides that the weary bucket o' bolts he is trying to unload on you was formerly owned by an elderly couple in Pasadena, who "only took it out of the garage on Sundays". Salesmen no longer foist this spiel on you—too many customers have heard about it. Just the same, my MG (a late 1950 Model TD) came from a retired Pasadena railroad man who actually drove it very little—about 5,000 miles. What he did do was take the car (at 4,000 miles) to McAfee Engineering Company for modifications: 8.6:1 compression ratio; larger valves; stronger valve springs; porting and polishing of the head; and a straight through muffler.

At 21,000 miles I sold the car to a close friend—Mr. Milton Eliades—who put the remaining 14,000 miles on the odometer. Milton, who invariably announces his several-times-weekly visits with a full-bore, second-gear, tire screaming, victory circle in front of my home, has kept a careful record of maintenance. This, along with my records, affords a clear picture of the car's history.

The McAfee stage of tune provided acceleration decidedly superior to those stock MG's I tangled with—though a frustrating misfire appeared at 4600 rpm. It developed that the feet on the bottom of the removable half of the aircleaner were bent, due to overtightening of the wingnut. Straightening these and filling the air cleaner to just below the indicated level with the lightest engine oil, provided acceleration to well over 7,000 *indicated* rpm (if I dared) in the first three gears, with 5500 *actual* rpm in fourth gear under all but unfavorable conditions.

The straight-through muffler may or may not have helped performance (MG Company says not), but it gave a reassuring sports car sound out the back, and an annoying, hollow, drumming with the top and side cur-

tains erected (A carpet-pad laid on the wood floor, back of the seat muffled this noise considerably). Speaking of the top, it is without question the sturdiest piece of cloth I have yet seen. Of but one thickness, it is still waterproof in its third year of use, though faded almost pure white from exposure and frequent scrubbings.

The MG's fastest speed (over a timed ¼ mile) was 83.3 mph—a long run with the top down, windshield folded flat, and a full tonneau cover in place. The tachometer, at this speed, read 6200 rpm—correction for error making it 5770. Shortly after this (21,000 miles) the head was removed and de-carbonized, and the valves were ground—producing a startling difference in performance (a timed run has not been made since).

American-made tappets had been installed at 4,000 miles, but they became noisy almost at once, and by 11,000 miles were unbearably loud. In 1951 certain MG parts were hard to come by, but I finally found four used and four new stock tappets which ran trouble free for the next 10,000. At that point a set of locally produced (and very light) cup-type tappets and matching pushrods gave a two-second acceleration improvement between 2000 and 4000 rpm, but they only lasted 1,000 miles before the pushrods came apart. A new set of the same lasted 300 miles and was replaced by the new graphite-impregnated stock MG tappets. These haven't run enough miles to allow a full report.

I had been advised by several authorities to drain the heavy duty oil from the engine in favor of Valvoline #30; it being felt that oils 'heavy with additives hadn't a proper viscosity for the high unit pressure of the MG cam. The stock tappets gave no trouble using Valvoline, but no oil seemed to help the non-stock components. At 35,000 miles the engine only consumes a little over one quart per 1,000 miles in normal driving; about twice that in fast highway cruising.

A nationally advertised additive for which fantastic claims are made was put into the gearbox and rear axle at 5,000 miles. The shift lever was thereupon easier to manipulate at first, but soon got "sticky", and the gears became noisy. The transmission and axle were drained immediately, which

stopped the noise, and an analysis broke the additive down to some 80% kerosene and a small percentage of low friction (but highly corrosive) soap substance. On a high speed run soon after this the gear lever stuck in 4th gear, which may or may not have been caused by the additive.

I always drove the MG strictly for fun: severe braking, accelerating and cornering. Yet the tires ran 29,029 miles—in spite of two crooked wheels, which certainly caused premature wear. At 29,000 new Firestone Deluxe Champions were fitted, but a cursory glance at 35,000 indicates that the original pure rubber Dunlops were as good if not better. Why the wheels bent, I can't really say. Perhaps it was my habit of jumping the car off the ground whenever the proper dip in the road presented itself. Straightening the wheels cost $2.00 each.

The MG's sensitive steering is marvelous, but to maintain the peak efficiency, I found it best to switch the tires around every 5,000 miles; and the wheels needed balancing somewhere between 6 and 10,000 miles. One garage did a wheel balance job for me and on a subsequent trip the MG was all over the road. I stopped and had the job re-done en route. Two handsfull of lead balancing weights were removed and the balance machine showed a better reading than it had with the weights on.

Every 10/15,000 miles the rear spring bolts were checked for tightness, for when loose, they spoiled high speed, straightaway steering by causing sideway in the rear end. With these minor attentions to wheel balance and spring tightness, the MG was a wonder for cruising out on the road. It always furnished a smooth-as-glass ride, and my wife and I were several times able to spend ten hours in the car on trips, with a remarkably low fatigue figure. Though the MG has a firm ride compared to the average family sedan, the seats are comfortable and there is plenty of room to stretch your legs. There is no pitch and roll on the straight, no lurching on corners, and severe braking does not throw one forward as is the case in the family sedan with its high, bench type seats.

Surprisingly little engine maintenance has been necessary in the 35,000. Nearly all the mechanical failures were the result of deviations from stock components, or from my habit of tinkering with the car when it was already running well. The fuel lines leading to the carburetors did not stand up too satisfactorily (our fuel?), but replacements of neoprene (at $1.50 each) are still going strong. Many early TDs had a tendency to leak wheel bearing grease. Mine started this at 12,000 miles—probably a sign that the bearings needed re-packing. Packing the wheels with Pennzoil wheel bearing lubricant solved the problem. The side curtain windows yellowed and scratched and were replaced at 20,000 miles—at a cost of $12.00 —but the leather in the seats is exceptionally durable when wiped over occasionally with Lexol, or some such preservative.

The generator, starter, and other electrical components have never given a moment's trouble, though I do prefer the American instrument light bulbs to Lucas—their light is whiter, and in my case they lasted longer. The battery needed replacing after two years, but in talking to other MG owners, I have yet to find another failure that early.

The biggest repair job of all I have not mentioned. It consisted of replacing the left front suspension (including wheel, tire, and brake), fender, radiator shell, and repairing the hood and frame. The MG, waiting to make a left turn, had been caught like a sitting duck by a stolen Chevrolet.

All told, the MG saved me money, was more fun to own and drive, and was as durable as any car I've ever owned. —DEARBORN

It is an odd thing that, after driving a test car for only a hundred or two miles, the temporary ownership assumes a feeling of permanence. Whatever the car, one drives along thinking up dozens of sound reasons for imagining that particular vehicle to be the best and most suitable for one's purposes. One does not, however, have to talk oneself into liking the Midget. I was under no misapprehensions about the M.G.'s place in the motoring picture. The Road Test had shown it to have a fair turn of speed, a maximum of 78 m.p.h. being recorded in favourable circumstances on two occasions. Not a very high maximum, the diehards will say, but one good enough for an engine of only 1¼ litres, pulling a not particularly light car that will do the shopping, sally forth with its occupants warm and dry in the foulest weather, and provide adequately for both sporting and non-sporting owners. Added to this, the glances which its pleasing appearance produces from passers-by pander to the very human failing of enjoyment at being envied.

Night Start

We were due to leave the start of the Edinburgh, the Rouncil Towers Motel, Kenilworth, at 12.15 a.m. on Whit Saturday morning. On Friday evening we left London and pointed the pleasantly long bonnet towards Leamington Spa. Here a meal was provided by friends, and at 11.15 we left, in steady rain and escorted by our host's Standard Vanguard (he knew the way), to the start. In an atmosphere of damp competitors trying to look nonchalant as they checked tyre pressures, oil, water and petrol, and attached rally number plates to their cars, we, too, tried to give the

TALKING

With umbrella at the ready a marshal prepares to time the M.G. in the test at Talla Linn in the Edinburgh Rally.

SO many people, to whom motoring means more than just getting around with the minimum of effort, are inclined to class the M.G. Midget vaguely as a sports car—a classification which includes such potent machinery as Ferrari, Alfa Romeo and suchlike—and to discuss and criticize its general performance, subconsciously at any rate, in terms of these vastly different cars. This is, of course, grossly unfair. Because the Chinese are able to produce soup from some sort of indigenous bird's nests, even Mrs. Beeton, the Ascari of the kitchen, could not be expected to boil up a sparrow's nest and produce the same result.

In the hands of the less wealthy, to whom an active participation in motoring sport is a "must," the M.G. can—and does—compete successfully in a wide variety of events all over the world. For the less ambitious—and there are thousands of them—who like their motoring to be in the open air when the weather permits, it provides a light-hearted, lively and tractable car which, above all, is fun to drive. The principal appeal, however, to its many adherents, is the comparatively modest price at which it does all this.

After a Road Test had been carried out on an example of the current model (*The Autocar*, May 5, 1953), the news that the use of the car had been extended for the M.C.C. Edinburgh Rally came as particularly pleasant news. A subsequent remark, "No doubt your experience of the car during the road test will help you to win a premier award," was less encouraging; the fact that no better than a "silver" resulted was, however, not the fault of the car. It was pleasant, though, to have the opportunity of extensive use of a car that had already proved itself to be well worthy of its manufacturer's slogan "Safety Fast."

Looking like "Mrs. Michelin," the navigator climbs into the car before the move away from the Carlisle lunch stop.

impression of hardened rallyists. Eventually we were sent on our way by a bedraggled marshal who remarked that he'd rather be sitting in the M.G.'s dry cockpit than getting drenched as he was. We agreed heartily, wished him good night and splashed out into the darkness.

The run to Harrogate, the breakfast stop, was pleasantly spent behind the subdued glow of the panel lighting and the car's adequate head lamps. Although there is bound to be a sensation of being "boxed in" when driving a two-seater with side screens that cannot be wound down at will, the flaps at the bottom of each screen tend to reduce this feeling of being cut off from the outside world. In the absence of traffic indicators these flaps are necessary for signalling. They are not, however, entirely convenient and the use of hand signals was abandoned in favour of a more than usually keen lookout in the driving mirror.

The route from Kenilworth to Harrogate was left to individual taste and a period of 4¾ hours was allowed for the 145-mile run. By driving normally and with no attempt to hurry, it was found that, despite the dark and rain, an average of 35 m.p.h. was easily maintained. The result was that considerable time was profitably "lost" by sleeping outside the Harrogate control.

After breakfast, the next section, leading to the lunch stop at Carlisle, gave ample opportunity of sampling the M.G.'s agility to the full. The route left main roads and wandered off across the Pennines through Oughtershaw, Buttertubs, Tan Hill, Hardknott, and Wrynose passes. This section included tests among which were a braking test on Buttertubs, and a stop-and-restart on a very steep climb following one of Hardknott's many hairpins. A period of three seconds was allowed in which to get away from the "stop astride" line and, as we arrived, a competitor in a sedate family saloon was gallantly burning out his clutch. The marshal cheerfully informed us that nearly 75 per cent of the entry had failed so far, though the M.G.s had nearly all managed it. After a long delay during which spectators pushed a predecessor up the hill, we took our turn. The hand brake, which works on the back wheels only, easily held the car on the steep section and, at the signal to start, the M.G. moved off without any trouble. The fly-off type, conveniently placed between the seats, is a blessing for manœuvres of this sort.

Ammeter, combined oil pressure and water temperature gauges, and the 5in rev counter and speedometer are all grouped in front of the driver. This is one of the detail points that make the Midget pleasing to drive.

roads were good and fairly empty, and there were niggling thoughts of those remarks about a first-class award.

During this part of the run the cornering and handling of the car came into their own and were much appreciated —as, indeed, were all its capabilities. The light and very accurate steering was a joy and there was no perceptible roll when cornering fast; the only indication that the car was being driven harder than usual was a considerable squeal from the tyres, which, unless pressures are kept two or three pounds above normal, can be annoying. Non-technical passers-by would no doubt attribute the squeal

T D . . . . .   MINIMS ON A MIDGET   by PETER GARNIER

On the return journey the M.G. took on the role of a fly-paper; the windscreen was as bad as the registration plate shown here and the absence of a bug deflector was regretted.

Queueing up outside the time check at Penicuik before reaching the finish at Edinburgh. The notice on the farther telegraph pole indicates the distance from the check.

From here the route led on towards Wrynose—a slow section with endless hairpins and a none too good surface. Considerable delay had been caused by the succession of failures on the stop-and-restart and, when a distance of 37 miles separated us from the Carlisle control, we calculated to our horror that we had only 39 minutes in which to get there. Arrival at this control over 10 minutes late automatically doomed one to failure, so we had a maximum of 49 minutes in which to cover the 37 miles and still qualify for a third-class award. The ten minutes grace was ignored—after all, the M.G. could do nearly 80 m.p.h., the

to excessive speeds rather than i.f.s. and condemn the driver, along with all his fellows, as being a road hog. The oversteer experienced with the recommended tyre pressures was greatly reduced by the slight pressure increase. Inevitably, with the ideally placed short, central gear lever, the temptation to use third gear is great, so crisp and easy is the change down. For accelerating fast out of corners, this gear is excellent and the revs build up quickly to 5,000.

On one straight stretch of road leading into Carlisle with the speedometer indicating 78 m.p.h. we were rapidly catching up an elderly Austin Seven which, without warning,

TALKING TD
. . . continued

In this form, with the hood down and the rigid, metal framed sidescreens in position, there is practically no draught. The M.G.'s pleasant lines—in effect a survival from the past—are well shown from this angle.

suddenly shed a large piece of cast iron, shaped like a flat banana, which bounced into the middle of the road. There was no opportunity to swerve and our right-side front wheel threw it up with an almighty bang somewhere under the M.G. To stop would have meant our efforts had been wasted, so as everything mechanical seemed to be all right we drove on. The speedometer was kept around the 80 m.p.h. mark for longish periods on this fast stretch, and at no time did the engine show any signs of overheating or objection. Eventually we drew up at the Carlisle control, two minutes late, having covered 37 miles in 41 minutes. We inspected for possible damage caused by the Austin's unwanted casting, and found a bump on the right-side running board about ⅛in high. Had the running board been made of aluminium it would almost certainly have been pierced.

In the Lowlands

From Carlisle onwards, to the finish at Edinburgh, the journey resumed the gentle country drive nature of the previous night's run. Two further tests were included; an acceleration test at Talla Linn and, at the finish in Edinburgh, a series of three stops and restarts against the clock. The lines astride which we had to stop were just a little too far apart for comfort in first gear and yet were too close for even the quickest change up into second. As a result, the M.G.'s rev counter sailed up to 6,000 r.p.m., where it was held until violent braking brought the car to rest astride the next line. In the earlier stages of the event the engine might have been spared such treatment, but this was the finish and it was not worth spoiling the ship for even a shilling or two's worth of tar. Apart from slight valve bounce the

M.G. stood this treatment without protest, after which we drove to the finish, handed in the number plates, and signed off.

A total distance of 457 miles had been covered, entailing nearly 18 hours—with the exception of meal stops—at the wheel. Many miles of very hilly country had been covered and violent braking and acceleration had been indulged in without thought for the car. At no time had the M.G. faltered nor had the brakes shown any signs of fade; at the finish they would still stop the car quickly in a straight line and there was no serious increase in pedal travel. The total petrol consumption had been in the order of 26 m.p.g. and the driving, right up to the finish, had been beguiling all the way. And, after this lengthy period in the car we were neither ditry, wet, nor unduly travel-weary; that no signs of soreness or stiffness were felt is an indication of the comfort and good driving position.

Now what does all this mean? Considered in terms of what the car sets out to do it achieves its purpose to a surprising degree. It is capable of standing up to harsh treatment without any ill effects. If the performance is not sufficient for the requirements of some sporting owners, this, too, can be coped with by means of the stage by stage tuning that can be carried out under the guidance of the manufacturer. It is not difficult to understand why the Midget, produced in an unbroken series over a period of 25 years, should still hold the appeal that it does, nor that such an astonishingly high percentage of the output should be sold in America.

It was very reluctantly that the car was driven back to Cowley on the following day—a further 360-odd miles—and returned to the manufacturers on Whit Monday, as sound and endearing as it had been when it left them.

The M.G. and crew at 8.35 a.m., 208 miles from the start, during the regularity test at Tan Hill, in the Lake District, where a heavy drizzle was falling.

A1 has frustrations apart from the "heavies"; the return journey to Cowley was held up by this level crossing at Leeming Bar, north of Boroughbridge in Yorkshire.

ROAD TESTING THE
LAYSTALL-LUCAS HEAD

Early in 1953 the well-known British firm, Laystall Engineering Company Ltd., announced a new aluminum alloy cylinder head, designed to fit any MG TC or TD engine and claimed to give a power increase of 20%. These heads are now available in the USA, and the object of this road test was to ascertain the exact amount of performance gain which an average owner could expect.

The first step was to obtain an absolutely stock MG TD in "average" condition. International Motors of Los Angeles loaned us such a car, having 14,500 miles on the odometer. The car was given a tune up and completed our usual full scale road test involving a little over 300 miles. The car did not come up to the performance recorded

by our Service Editor's car (Road and Track, February '53), so as a further check we ran an abbreviated test on another car which happens to belong to the Tech. Ed's brother. This second car had 11,000 miles on the odometer and has been very carefully maintained and tuned. Its performance was fractionally slower than the International Motors car.

Having established a base line performance that agrees very closely to data published in England, the first car was returned to International Motors for installation of the Laystall-Lucas cylinder head. Aside from new spark plugs, there was no other change.

A full scale road test was then made on the same car as originally, with only

the new cylinder head added. The performance data recorded here in both tabular and graphic form shows that there is a very considerable improvement in all around performance and that the Laystall-Lucas head actually gives better performance than the Mark II engine, even with the stock 1¼" SU carburetors. (The Mark II and the new TF have 1½" carburetors.)

Since power required increases as the square of the speed, the gain in top speed of approximately 11 mph shows that the power has been increased by at least 30%. Furthermore, the Tapley readings recorded indicate that the torque is over 11% better than stock.

How is all this accomplished with only a new cylinder head assembly?

Solid line shows the improved performance of the Laystall-MG.   Useful chart shows the excellent spacing of the MG gear ratios.

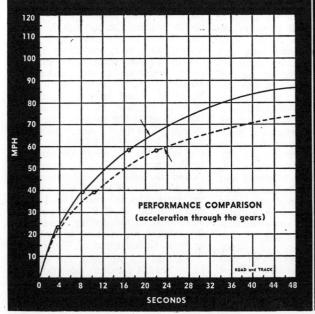

PERFORMANCE COMPARISON
(acceleration through the gears)

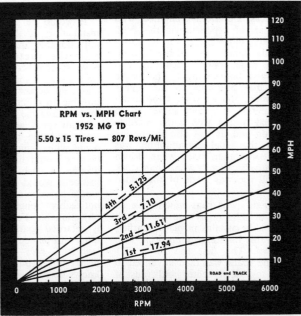

RPM vs. MPH Chart
1952 MG TD
5.50 x 15 Tires — 807 Revs/Mi.

4th — 5.125
3rd — 7.10
2nd — 11.61
1st — 17.94

ROAD and TRACK ROAD TEST No. F-1-54

MG - TD -- Laystall Comparison

STOCK SPECIFICATIONS

Wheelbase	94.0 in.	Horsepower	54.4
Tread, front	47.4 in.	peaking speed	5200
rear	50.0 in.	equivalent mph	75.0
Tire size	5.50 x 15	Torque, ft/lbs.	63.5
Curb weight	2015 lbs.	peaking speed	2600
distribution	50/50	equivalent mph	37.4
Test weight	2355 lbs.	Mph per 1000 rpm	14.4
Engine	4 cyl.	Mph at 2500 fpm	
Valves	ohv	piston speed	61.5
Bore and stroke	2.62 x 3.54	Gear ratios (overall)	
Displacement	76.3 cu in.	4th	5.12
	(1250 cc)	3rd	7.10
Compression ratio	7.25	2nd	10.61
R & T performance factor	37.9	1st	17.94

PERFORMANCE

	Stock	Laystall
Top speed (avg.)	77.0	87.9
fastest one way	77.6	89.1
Max. speed in gears—		
3rd	61	65
2nd	40	43
1st	24	26
Shift points from—		
3rd	58	58
2nd	39	39
1st	23	23
Speedometer error	4% fast	

ACCELERATION

	Time in Seconds	
	Stock	Laystall
0-30 mph	6.0	5.2
0-40 mph	11.2	8.4
0-50 mph	16.0	12.5
0-60 mph	24.1	18.0
0-70 mph	39.0	25.1
0-80 mph	—	34.9
Standing ¼ mile		
average	23.5	20.9
best	23.2	20.8
Mileage—mpg	22/25	21/26

TAPLEY READINGS

	Lbs/ton at Mph	
Gear	Stock	Laystall
1st	440 at 21	500 at 20
2nd	360 at 31	400 at 29
3rd	242 at 36	270 at 34
4th	175 at 40	195 at 38

COASTING
(wind and rolling resistance)

	Lbs/ton	
	Stock	Laystall
10 mph	15	15
30 mph	35	35
60 mph	100	100

First of all, the compression ratio is 9.3 to 1, compared to the stock 7.25 or the 8.10 of the Mark II. The oversize valves and heavier valve springs which are included in the "package" are, of course, stock Mark II parts and contribute to the overall effect. The ports match the stock MG manifolds but have been redesigned in size and shape—the result of very extensive and thorough flow bench testing by Mr. John Lucas, a consulting engineer with many years of experience in this field.

The 30% bhp increase can be attributed to the combination of higher compression ratio, better breathing and higher valve bounce speed. The torque gain is due primarily to the higher compression, and we suspect the smaller carburetors contribute something to low speed torque with some sacrifice at the top end. It was also interesting to note that fuel consumption was slightly better than stock when driven conservatively, slightly worse than stock when full use was made of the added performance.

The high speed runs which gave an average of 87.9 mph were made with top and side curtains in place. Earlier, we tried this Laystall-equipped car with top down. The first run gave 73.1 mph! The spark was then advanced to exactly top dead center and runs at 86.6 and 85.8 were recorded. Then the top and side curtains were set up, giving a further speed increase of 2.2 mph.

During the acceleration checks, we found little or no advantage in exceeding 5500 rpm through the gears on either car, though the 150-lb valve springs supplied with the Laystall head allowed 6200 rpm without valve bounce. The zero to 60 mph time could be improved slightly by going to 5700 rpm, but when doing this, the standing ¼ mile and zero to 70 and 80 mph times were about the same.

It would be wrong to say that the installation of this head produces no objectionable qualities. If this were true, the factory would long ago have standardized on a 9.3 compression ratio. Though premium fuel of about 90 octane was used, it was impossible to eliminate low speed knock by retarding the spark. We experimented with spark advance throughout the tests, and the high speed runs were made with a higher setting than most owners would find acceptable for city driving. A dash controlled manual adjustment would be easy to install and would be very useful. The engine runs noticeably "rougher" though this is not objectionable. For traffic work, a slightly retarded spark gives smoother running with perceptible knocking only below 2000 rpm—and then only under nearly full throttle. A good driver, who knows how to use the gearbox, will not find the above drawback objectionable or disadvantageous in view of the added performance. The purpose of this

discussion is not to "knock" the Laystall head, but merely to point out that 9.3 to 1 is the top limit on compression ratios for the MG with available fuels and too high for lazy "never shift" drivers, or for 2nd gear starts.

In conclusion, it might be well to clarify certain widespread fallacies regarding high compression ratio. Contrary to what appears to be a widely held opinion, a higher compression ratio reduces the load imposed on the cooling system. The fact that the higher compression ratio extracts more useful work (power or torque) from a given amount of fuel means that less heat energy is lost via the water jackets and exhaust ports. However, when more bhp is being used, there is a higher rate of heat rejection. In other words, it takes about 22 bhp to propel the TD at 60 mph. With the 9.3 compression ratio it takes less fuel to propel the car at that speed than formerly. On the other hand, since the available added bhp exceeds the gain in fuel efficiency, there is a possibility of higher heat loads, if the extra bhp is used. The Laystall equipped car at 87.9 mph puts out more heat to the cooling system and the exhaust valves than the stock car at its maximum speed of 77.0 mph.

Summed up, we think the Laystall-Lucas head is excellent value (at $225) for those MG owners who want the extra performance and understand the minor disadvantageous.—J.B.

Used Cars on the Road—96

1953 M.G. TD

Basic price new	..	£530	0s 0d
Purchase tax	..	£221	19s 2d
Price secondhand	..	£525	0s 0d

Acceleration from rest through gears:

to 30 m.p.h.	..	5.6 sec.
to 50 m.p.h.	..	14.6 sec.
to 60 m.p.h.	..	22.6 sec.
20 to 40 m.p.h. (top gear):		9.9 sec.
30 to 50 m.p.h. (top gear):		11.1 sec.

Petrol consumption: 28-34 m.p.g.
Oil consumption: 2,000 m.p.g.
Speedometer reading: 24,594
Car first registered: May, 1953

The internal condition of the car was pleasing, and the carpets and trim had lasted well. The adjustable bench seat was comfortable, but the leather had aged more than the rest of the car

PARTICULAR care is required in the purchase of a second-hand sports car, for although such models often receive a generous share of care and maintenance, there is a danger that over-enthusiastic driving may have caused premature wear and depreciation. But under the bonnet of this M.G. there was no sign that the car had led any but a normal life, and there was nothing to indicate that it had had an especially arduous history.

The M.G. was provided for test by Performance Cars, Ltd., Great West Road, Brentford, Middlesex. Within a short time of collection it became obvious that its general condition was good for its age. There were points for criticism, but the depreciation was less than that normally found after three years' use.

The engine was creditably quiet, and the exhaust note, though pleasing and healthy, was not obtrusively loud. Similarly, the gear box noise was limited to an acceptable degree of whine, and the back axle was silent. The extent of free play in the transmission was less than the average.

Performance is a primary factor in such a car, and it was gratifying to find that, as often happens, the acceleration was a shade faster than that of the new car. However, engine abilities were considerably hampered by a clutch in which slip could easily be provoked. For normal driving, the clutch was satisfactory and there was no tendency towards judder. There was no slip when starting from rest in bottom gear; it occurred as fast upward changes were made when maximum acceleration was required.

It was necessary to depress the pedal fully to obtain a silent gear change, and even then it could not be hurried without producing a crunch from the mechanism. This was a pity because the tiny gear lever was a delight to handle. Single-declutched gear changes seem out of place on an M.G., but the synchromesh on the upper three ratios was effective for normal use.

The suspension is by independent coil springs at the front, and naturally tends to be on the firm side, but the ride was still very pleasant and there was no noticeable road rumble. From the low driving position, what pitching there was at the front end tended to be exaggerated, but the dampers were, in fact, very powerful. The silence of the suspension, even over really atrocious road surfaces, was commendable. There was never any bottoming as the wheels bumped over potholes. On rough roads there was an excessive degree of scuttle shake, sometimes so bad as to make it difficult to read the instruments accurately or to hold the steering steady; but on reasonable surfaces the car felt pleasantly solid.

Performance

Without over-stressing the engine, the wavering speedometer needle could be placed on the 80 m.p.h. mark, at which time the true speed was around 72 m.p.h. But the M.G.'s ability to hurry along at high average speeds was owed more to the excellent steering and good roadholding, together with brakes which were truly sufficient for the car's performance. The fly-off handbrake was also powerful and would hold the car on a considerable gradient.

The head light beam was adequate, but no more; however, two small Lucas spotlights had been added to the car, wired together through one switch. One of these gave a diffused spread of light, and the other a spot beam, and the combination was splendid for fast night driving when there was no oncoming traffic. Another addition to the car was the amber winking indicators which worked well, though the illuminated switch was masked somewhat by the steering wheel. All lights and instruments were working efficiently. Two external mirrors, chromium guards on the rear wings and the door tops, additional chromium strips forward of the running boards and a badge bar were other accessories added to the TD.

This is essentially a car for the enthusiast, and it is least of all intended for the motorist who values his comfort in winter. With the hood and sidescreens in position there were many rattles, and draughts came into the car in all directions. The hood fell below the standard of the rest of the car, and could be regarded only as an emergency device to keep most of the rain off. On the other hand, with the hood folded back in fine weather, the fresh-air motoring was delightful; at high speeds goggles were an advantage, and the tearing wind was most refreshing.

Underneath, the car was in very good condition and there was little rusting; the silencer appeared to be almost new. The car was also very well shod and should not need any tyre replacements for many miles. The toolkit was almost complete and in good condition.

M.G.s invariably command high prices on the used car market, and in return it is reasonable to expect to obtain a vehicle in first-class condition. There was certainly little at fault with this TD, and for the sporting motorist it is an admirable little car.

The M.G. looked very attractive in the red cellulose in which the body was finished. In one or two places there were signs of early rusting below the paint at some of the bodywork joints, but the finish was otherwise very good, and the chromium was excellent. The external appearance was marred only by the shabby canvas tonneau

"HOW will we get out of this?" ponders Rita as rear of MG sinks into a Turkish water trap.

BOMBAY-LONDON

10,000-mile honeymoon turned into a dust-and-mud moon, but was a great adventure, says Charles Rubin

THIS is the story of a belated honeymoon which took my wife, myself, and our 1950 MG TD 10,000 miles through Asia and Europe.

Rita and I were married in 1955 but were both flat broke then, and couldn't take the trip to Europe we'd promised ourselves until two years later.

And what a honeymoon it turned out to be! Dustmoon or mudmoon would be a better description—but a tremendous experience nevertheless.

With the red MG stowed securely in the ship's hold, we sailed from Sydney on March 5, disembarking at Bombay 18 days later. Two days spent chasing after permits and clearances, another day for sightseeing, and we were ready to push off.

Early Worries

The last night in Bombay I did not sleep much. Thinking of the 7000 miles to Western Europe, through countries I knew next to nothing about—except that it would not be possible to obtain spare parts —I got the jitters. The car had

CARAVAN in India means a line of heavily loaded elephants, not a van behind a car. But main hazards are cows, buffalo, and dreamy cyclists.

already done well over 50,000 miles; I know what makes a car go, but I am no mechanic. Maybe we were crazy to undertake such a trip.

But in the morning I had no time for these thoughts. The bellboy came up as we were dressing to inform me that somebody had run off with the wheels of our car during the night. I raced down to the MG, only to discover that the wheels were still on the car, but two hubcaps were missing. Then the night porter appeared and explained that thieves had tried to steal the hubcaps, but he had given chase and recovered them.

A clear case of blackmail, it seemed to me. After a generous (but reluctant) tip, the porter went inside and brought out the hubcaps.

It took a lot of fiddling to stow our

I slid out of the sleeping-bag and grabbed the torch: a truck had stopped on the road, and two figures were coming towards us. They stopped a short distance away, feeling no doubt as uneasy as ourselves. After exchanging a few muttered words they returned to the truck and drove off. As you can imagine, we didn't sleep much after that.

Most of the remaining nights in India and Pakistan we spent at the "resthouses" found in all the bigger villages. For a fixed nominal sum, they provide the traveller with a bed and reasonable washing facilities.

The road through India was good and we found petrol stations at regular intervals. The only real danger to the motorist in India comes from cows—and I don't mean because they are considered holy. Doing 50 m.p.h.,

VOYAGE began here — Rita and Charles Rubin on the "Gateway to India" in Bombay.

BY MG

luggage, of which we had too much —but finally everything was in place and we drove off.

I began to feel happy and carefree when we hit the open road. Except for an occasional caravan, and a truck now and again, we had the road to ourselves. The villages we passed through did not look at all inviting, so we decided to spend the first night camping. Driving a few yards off the road, we crept into our sleeping-bags — but sleep would not come. We were both too nervous, without admitting it to each other. When finally I did doze off a bit, my wife pushed me suddenly. "Somebody is coming," she whispered.

ODD sight in a Bombay park: the fairy-tale shoe that the old woman lived in, built to amuse children.

I would not like to hit even an unholy water-buffalo, which usually decides to cross the road just as you approach. After several close shaves I learned that it was no use honking—you have to slow down and go round the animal.

Another hazard was the frequently encountered cyclist, pedalling along dead in the middle of the road. When you honk one of these lads, anything is liable to happen: he may swing left, right, and maybe left again, or else fall off the bike from shock.

The amount an Indian can carry on his bicycle never ceased to amaze us. Big milk cans (two on each side) or perhaps a bed—and very often we saw up to four persons on one bike.

More Complications

We reached Delhi on April 1, with little petrol in the tank and only two rupees in my pocket. To our consternation, we found that on this day the Indians changed their monetary system, and all the banks were closed. Finally we located a kindly bank

LONDON is 5887 miles away, says this sign in Pakistan. Next "town" mentioned, Kila Safed, turned out to be one mud building — uninhabited.

rupees then, if his predictions came true?—he asked me. I promised him 100 rupees if everything turned out as he said. Meanwhile he accepted 5 rupees, which was his normal fee.

We liked New Delhi, with its modern shops and wide, tree-lined streets. We were particularly fascinated by an observatory built in 1725, which consists of six huge and mysterious masonry instruments used to determine the movements of the celestial bodies. Old Delhi is dominated by the "Red Fort," in which once stood the famous Peacock Throne, now housed in a museum in Tehran.

Next overnight stop was Lahore, and here we were alarmed by newspaper reports that a party of Americans and Iranian police had been murdered by brigands near the Pakistan border. We thought this might ruin our chances of a visa for Iran, which we hoped to obtain in Quetta.

manager who took us to a travel office and used his influence to get us some Indian currency in exchange for a traveller's cheque.

He then invited us to dinner. The rice-and-meat dish he fed us was tasty and did not seem too hot, but I guess we ate too much of this unfamilar cooking, for Rita was ill and spent the next day in bed.

Going to Delhi on my own, I fell into the hands of a soothsayer who startled me by giving me my name and date of birth on a slip of paper before I had a chance to tell him what they were; later he repeated the same trick with Rita's name and birth date. The next was just the usual stuff. He promised me a lot of money would come my way soon (I am still waiting) and foretold my return to India. Would I give him 50

THIS is a mountain "road" somewhere in Iran. When an Iranian says a road is good, it means a miserable track; "bad" means non-existent.

IRAN again, with Rita reconnoitring the numerous rain-water channels that cut up the road, middle of which is strewn with sump-busting rocks.

Luckily our fears were unfounded.

Between Multan and Subkur we came upon an old brick road the surface of which was badly broken up and often interrupted by dirt tracks. Progress became very slow and we ate a lot of dust. The rest of the way to Quetta was quite good, however. It led mostly through desert, straight and flat for miles, and I had to struggle to keep awake.

In Quetta, a clean, small town surrounded by mountains, we stayed only long enough to have the car serviced and to get our visas, which took one day. At a road fork not far from Quetta, a signboard informed us that it was only 5887 miles more to London. Next town was Nushki, where we stacked up with plenty of petrol and water, because ahead lay a long, lonely stretch.

About 20 miles from Nushki the road was broken up. I didn't see it in time, and the resut was that a big stone cracked the faithful MG's sump. In the process of stopping the flow of oil by tying rags round it I burnt my fingers, but we made it back to Nushki with still some oil left.

As there were no welding facilities, men from the local military post helped me patch up the hole with a piece of tin and rivets. The repair lasted all the way to Tehran, though we had to add a quart of oil every day.

Having negotiated the broken bitumen safely on our second attempt, we struck a reasonable gravel road—until this, too, deteriorated suddenly, about 100 miles from Pakistan's western border..

Iran Was Tougher Still

Then, at a place called Kila Safed on our map, the road petered out altogether. This was supposed to be the Pakistani border post, but all we could see was one big mud building, and not a soul anywhere.

There wasn't the faintest track to indicate the way ahead, over what looked like an immense, dry, rugged river-bed. Far away across it we could see an oasis dotted with a few

HUGE trucks carrying enormous loads of cotton bales became a familiar sight to the Rubins. Friendly truckies often helped them out of trouble.

The officials were friendly and treated us to tea and sweets. The 50 miles from Minjaveh to Zahedan consisted of a very hard road, interrupted by innumerable streamlets, and gave us a foretaste of what was to come.

From Zahedan to Tehran lead two routes—one through the desert, and a longer one through the mountains. The desert route was impassable, while the mountain road was described to me as very bad for the first 150 miles, but improving later on, as it reaches the more populated districts.

STOP for petrol always drew a crowd, whether in India, Pakistan, Iran or Turkey. RIGHT: Journey's end—the faithful MG on London's Tower Bridge.

white houses—but how to reach it?

Rita burst into tears, and I felt like doing the same, when two Iranian soldiers suddenly appeared before us. Waving a couple of shovels, they signalled us to follow.

The MG travelled a few yards and got stuck in a ditch. We dug it out and drove on at snail's pace, the soldiers levelling a track ahead with their shovels. Thus we reached the oasis of Minjaveh, which turned out to be the Iranian border post.

BOMBAY—LONDON

Now, when an Iranian says a road is good, it means it is a bad dirt track —and when he says it is bad, that means you won't find any road at all.

Due to abnormal rains in that area, there wasn't much left of the track for about 150 miles. However, apart from tearing off an overrider from the rear bumper bar, we got through all right. Then the so-called "good road" started—and this proved to be just one long nightmare.

Up and down it went, with an average of three rivers a day to cross. The usual procedure was for Rita to wade ahead, making sure there were no big stones in the way, and for me to follow (also getting wet feet, in spite of sitting in the car).

On the high plateaus the road was straight and flat, but so badly corrugated that I didn't dare do more than 25 m.p.h. Even so, everything on the car rattled, squeaked and banged. A tiny crack in the front mudguard, caused by hitting a large dog in Pakistan, measured over three inches by the time we reached Tehran.

There was a fairly steady traffic of tankers, buses and trucks, the drivers of which always pulled up to inquire if anything was wrong when we stopped to rest.

On the flats, the approach of one of these sturdily built vehicles was heralded by a cloud of dust which reduced visibility to zero for about a minute.

Whenever we stopped in a town to buy petrol and provisions, the car was surrounded by a crowd, and before long the police would arrive to keep them in check. The people were always good-natured, though. I only got mad at them when they twisted movable things on the car and tested the springs by moving it up and down.

We found we could always make ourselves understood with the help of gestures—or nearly always. In one village we could not convey the idea that we wanted milk, until Rita drew the hind part of a cow in the dust. I was afraid they would bring us half a cow, but we got the desired milk.

About 200 miles from Tehran a rear spring snapped right through with a terrific bang. A tanker driver helped me strap it up with a block of wood and rope, but next morning a front coil spring broke in two places. Nevertheless we reached Tehran that day, and never was the sight of a big city more welcome.

It had taken us five days—sometimes driving till late at night—to cover the 1057 miles from Zahedan. We had camped out every night and were unbelievably filthy. After my first bath in Tehran I had to scrape the dirt from the plughole with my fingers so that the water could drain.

Tehran to Turkey

The first three days in Tehran I spent under the car, taking off the sump, replacing it after it had been welded, taking down and refitting new springs (which had to be made as there were no original parts available) and tightening everything in sight. Surprisingly, the only other damage was a dented muffler.

One of the people we met in Tehran advised us to go to Tabriz via Resht. It would be well worth the extra miles, they assured me, as the road was better and the country beautiful.

It was beautiful all right, driving from Resht along the Caspian seashore, and the road not quite so bad either—but to get there we first had to negotiate a shocking 100-mile stretch, where the front spring renewed in Tehran collapsed again. I had it welded and eventually went as far as Vienna with the car lopsided.

Then, about 20 miles from Astara, Iranian soldiers turned us back because we had no permit to enter the Russian border zone. What I thought of this at the time is unprintable. It took a good day to get back to Kasvin, through which we had passed two days ago!

From there the road was worse than ever—and the dust was now replaced by mud. Late one afternoon we came to a forced halt at a river which was deeper than any we had crossed before. But the real danger was the strong current, which nearly swept me off my feet when I tested it.

Again a tanker came to our rescue: the driver offered to tow us through. I was very scared but decided to take the risk, as there was no other way. We tied a short wire rope to the bumper bar and fastened it at the back of the tanker.

The actual crossing took perhaps half a minute, but it was the most exciting half-minute of the whole trip. Only a few yards from shore, I could feel water round my feet; something scraped and banged underneath, and then the MG began to move sideways. I was getting thoroughly alarmed when, suddenly, the big wheels of the tanker in front of me lifted themselves out of the water and we were on dry land again.

A look under the car showed everything in order, except that the exhaust pipe and muffler were a bit more bashed in. The engine fired at first try. The driver made us understand that another deep river lay ahead, and that he would wait there to tow us through again if necessary; but this time we made it on our own.

The last day in Iran I drove till one a.m. and then stopped only because I could not find the way out of a dried-out river bed. Rita had been asleep for a long time; I rested my head on the steering wheel and fol-

lowed her example.

At noon next day we had Iran behind us.

Turkey Was Wet

The road into Turkey was also only a dirt track, but its surface was even and we were able to maintain a good speed. It was wonderful to feel the wind rush around a fast-moving car again, and not be forced to make incessant gear-changes.

But alas—at 4 p.m. we ran out of petrol, and when a truck did come along after a half-hour wait, it turned out to be a diesel. The driver said there was a village with a petrol station about three miles ahead, so I took our two-gallon can and started walking.

One hour later the village came in sight. From where I saw it, the road made a big bend which I decided to cut. That meant I had to cross a stream which looked narrow enough to jump over at that distance—but not so when I got to it.

I managed to throw the can to the opposite bank, then hitched up my pants, took the shoes in my hand and started wading. When only a couple of yards separated me from the opposite shore, I stepped into a hole and was in water up to my hips. Dripping wet, and miserable as could be, I limped in my wet shoes into the village.

The petrol attendant wouldn't take any pounds but accepted a ten-dollar bill. While arguing about what I should get for my dollars, I saw a truck going in the direction of Rita and the MG; hailing the driver, I got a lift back and felt a lot better after changing into dry socks and shoes.

Dead-beat by the time we reached Agri, we spent the night at the first hotel we saw. In the morning we again struck currency trouble. The banks wouldn't cash our traveller's cheques, and no one wanted our pound-sterling notes. We finally sold Rita's watch to enable us to carry on.

In Erzurum I sold a cheque to a black-market guy at the hotel so that we could continue the next day, which was a Sunday. A few miles out of town we came to a river crossing and promptly got stuck, with the front of the chassis resting on a sandbank and the rear wheels digging themselves in.

The three driving lessons my wife once had came in handy now. With her reversing and me pushing, we got the car out, then filled the hole with stones and crossed successfully. But our sleeping-bags had got wet and we couldn't use them for the next three nights, which we spent freezing in the car.

All that time it never stopped raining, and the road became one slippery mass. We kept ploughing through mud, hoping for the best. Time and again, at steeper inclines, I had to let the car run back and start again with a good run-up in first gear. There was nothing solid for the tyres to get a grip on. Up and down the mountainsides we slithered, the rain turning to snow whenever we neared a crest.

One morning the brakes suddenly seized. For two hours I worked in drizzling rain, with Rita holding the umbrella over me when it got too heavy. The trouble lay in the master-cylinder, which had so much dirt in it that it wouldn't work properly. Finally I freed up the system by loosening the brake adjustments a little.

In the afternoon of the same day, on a stretch which looked like a churned-up paddock, a truck came towards us. When he had almost passed us, some part on the back of his tray hit the windscreen support of our MG, cracking the screen. Rita burst into tears, and I felt very upset too—especially when the driver stuck his head out of the cabin and gave us a malicious wave.

With our spirits below zero and the temperature not much above it, we skidded on. But after Sivas conditions improved: the sun shone again, and our spirits rose as we neared Europe.

We stayed only half a day in Ankara, and reached Istanbul the following evening. Three wonderful days we stayed in Istanbul, which, in spite of its modern life, reminds you at every step of the legendary East.

The remaining few miles through Turkey were covered without incident, and the potholed roads of Greece and Yugoslavia seemed quite smooth after our previous experiences.

Once we had got to Austria the rest of the journey was a sheer picnic. We spent two months in Vienna, staying with some old friends of mine (I was born there and didn't come to Australia till 1949). The MG, fitted with new front springs and a new master-cylinder, looked more like its old self once more. In fact, things couldn't have been better—except that we had very little money left.

Setting off again on the last stage across Europe, we reached London on July 24. We had been on the road for nearly four months and had clocked just under 10,000 miles in 41 days' driving—an average of about 240 miles a day.

Not bad, considering all the difficulties. My hat's off to the faithful old MG—here's hoping we stay together for a long time.

FOOTNOTE: Since writing this, Charles Rubin has taken to the road again with his M.G., but this time without Rita. At present he is in Iran, where he got a temporary job to build up his capital. But he'll soon be off once more, and it looks as though the old soothsayer who predicted that he would return to India knew something, after all. ● ● ●

CONTINUED FROM PAGE 73

The Arnolt Corporation, which up to now has made a good thing of MG accessories, has recently announced an MG coupe and a convertible. These cars carry Italian coachwork of a high order and retail for about $3500. A few years ago the Arnolt would have been as popular as a blonde on a desert island but, at this stage, I can't help thinking of the Porsche in the same price range and possessing near-Jaguar performance. We'll see about that, but in the meantime it's safe to forecast a happy future for the less expensive versions.   ☆ ☆

FRONT END: The Mark II TD M.G. has air scoops to the 2LS brake-drums, rack and pinion steering and Andrex dampers on the helical and wishbones i.f.s.

The TD Midget Mark II
CONTINUED FROM PAGE 23

luggage rack is available, and the eleven-gallon tank will be appreciated for such work. The hood and sidescreens really do give saloon comfort, and the hood disappears when not in use. There is a neat locker for the sidescreens, but they are rather a tight fit and need care in stowing. The headlamps are mounted fairly high, and permit fast driving at night.

As can be seen from the data

panel, there is plenty of acceleration and the mean timed speed of 88 m.p.h. is excellent. The highest speed I obtained during the test was 92 m.p.h., but 90 m.p.h. was a commonplace, and I put the car round some bends at the latter velocity. A friend, watching this proceeding from the side of the road, reported that the "TD" looked steady and under full control.

Except for disc wheels and bumpers, the appearance is entirely traditional. The makers are obviously correct in retaining the "old look", for this is a best-seller, and a mighty dollar-earner to boot. It is a well proportioned car, and will entirely satisfy the very many customers who like an M.G. to look like an M.G. Nevertheless, the fine performance which it gives in its present form makes one wonder what a lighter and more aerodynamic version would do. No doubt the factory is far too busy, though, for any thought of an additional model to be entertained, and I expect the "TD" will be in full production for years to come.

In a few words, then, this is a car which will make many new friends for the marque without alienating any of the old ones. It is the best all-rounder that has yet come out of Abingdon.

JOHN BOLSTER.

90

USED CARS
on the Road

No. 181   1952 M.G. TD

PRICE: Secondhand £345; New—basic £530, with tax £826

Petrol consumption 24-29 m.p.g.	Date first registered 3 December 1952
Oil consumption 220 m.p. pint	Mileometer reading 79,702

FROM a financial point of view, this is a good time of the year for the purchase of a used sports car. Inevitably, with the onset of winter, interest in this section of the market is dull, and dealers saddled with sports cars among their stock are generally ready to compromise with buyers over terms and prices. Bearing this in mind, the price of £345 asked for this nine-year-old M.G. TD may seem high, but allowance must be made for its unusually good condition.

A reconditioned engine has been fitted and is in good form. Starting is reliable, and there is all (and more) of the crispness and response to the throttle associated with the model; this favourable impression is confirmed by the clean under-bonnet appearance. The gearing of the TD is fairly low, but the engine does not object to use of reasonably high revs. In top gear a

severe vibration of the gear lever occurred at speeds higher than 5,300 r.p.m., corresponding to 77 m.p.h., but at lower speeds both engine and transmission remain smooth.

Wear has nearly eliminated all traces of synchromesh from the gearbox, but no doubt there are many among potential buyers who would prefer it this way, particularly since the change itself has lost none of its original precision. Clutch take-up is unexpectedly sudden on first acquaintance, but with familiarity the driver is soon able to take off perfectly smoothly in bottom gear with quite high engine revs.

Despite a mileage of nearly 80,000, the rack-and-pinion steering remains the best point of the car, and is entirely in character, having complete freedom from lost movement as well as being pleasantly light to operate. Tremor on rough surfaces is notably absent. The suspension is extremely firm without being actually harsh, so that although the occupants are well aware of road surface conditions the car does not hop about. In hard cornering the M.G. is delightfully stable.

A slight tendency for the brakes to pull to the right is the only fault which might justify attention, though the efficiency of the brakes and their powerful response to the pedal are not affected. The handbrake is effective and convenient to use.

As is only to be expected, much evidence of wear is given by the well-creased seats, which are a combination of individual cushions with a one-piece bench backrest. The facia and interior trim have become somewhat marked, but in most respects the interior appearance of the M.G. is particularly good in rela-

tion to age and the mileage covered. Similarly, the black paintwork is in very good shape, and gives a well-preserved appearance to the exterior. One headlamp and the sidelamps show extensive scratching, but elsewhere the chrome has lasted well, and the windscreen frame and radiator are unmarked.

To add to the good exterior condition, a new beige hood and complete set of sidescreens have been supplied. The only let-down is a somewhat shabby tonneau cover but the zip failed on this during the test, and possibly Baker and Roger will "throw in" a new tonneau cover when the car is sold. As applied to the M.G. TD, the hood and sidescreens are particularly barbarous, with much daylight visible around the frames from inside, but when all are in place, surprisingly little draught enters the car even at speed; and with the useful warmth blown back from the engine and gearbox the interior remains quite snug, despite the lack of a heater.

Accessories added to the M.G. are a passenger's map-reading light on the facia, two wing mirrors, a Tudor windscreen washer which is working well and a large reversing lamp, which is out of action. There is also a strip demister in the toolbox under the bonnet, and a useful feature is that the car has been equipped with winking indicators. They are operated by a non-self-cancelling facia control; the M.G. also has a luggage grid.

Lying on the back of the sensible 12½-gallon slab fuel tank is the spare wheel, with a well-worn Dunlop cover. The wheels on the road have Michelin X, about two-thirds worn at the front, yet nearly new on the rear. A jack and wheel-nut spanner comprise the only items of toolkit, and there is a starting handle in clips on the rear of the seat backrest.

Like the rest of the car, the chassis and underbody bear evidence of being well-preserved, and there is commendably little corrosion. The undersides of the front wings are painted red.

The M.G. TD is a splendid little sports car, tremendous fun to drive, and a pleasant reminder of the immediate post-war era. Of the car tested, the most appropriate summary was made by a complete stranger at a garage, who commented that it "seemed to have had a good home." We replied that there had, in fact, been four homes, but agreed that they certainly must have been good ones.

A dipping mirror is fitted, but at speed it vibrates and is of little value. The seats are quite well shaped and give comfortable support; visibility over the tapering bonnet and the twin domes of the headlamps, is good. All equipment including the clock in the rev. counter is working

PERFORMANCE CHECK
(Figures in brackets are those of the original Road Test, 15 May 1953)

0 to 30 m.p.h. ..5·9 sec (6·3)	Standing quarter-mile ..22·4 sec (23·4)
0 to 50 m.p.h...13·4 sec (15·6)	
0 to 60 m.p.h...20·0 sec (23·9)	20 to 40 m.p.h. (top gear).. 8·4 sec (12·4)
0 to 70 m.p.h...30·3 sec (39·6)	30 to 50 m.p.h. (top gear).. 8·6 sec (12·6)

Provided for test by Baker and Roger Ltd.,
170, High Street South, Dunstable, Bedfordshire
Telephone: Dunstable 62575

For years
the most
consistently
successful
sports car
in the world

Safety **MG** *fast !*

THE M.G. CAR COMPANY LIMITED, SALES DIVISION, COWLEY, OXFORD

London Showroom : University Motors Ltd., Stratton House, 80 Piccadilly, W.1
Overseas Business: Nuffield Exports Ltd., Oxford and 41 Piccadilly, London, W.1

"Have I thought of anything except another TD? Well, no..."

MG TD

The One In Between

Some say the TD is the least auspicious of the best known Abingdon trio, TC, TD and TF. But GEOFF BEWLEY disagrees — and he's owned two of them.

I WAS WALKING down to the Bondi Beach newsagent's on a Saturday morning when I saw the yellow MG TD parked in a row of cars down the side of one of the service stations on the corner. It had a deep gash across the front of its right mudguard, but otherwise it appeared to be in good condition. I was thinking what a pity it was about the damage to the mudguard when one of the garage attendants came over.

"Are you interested in this one?" he asked me.

"I don't know," I said. "Is it for sale?"

"We're trying to get rid of it," he said. "It belonged to this Canadian bloke and he had it restored, and then he got into a smash just before he went back home to Canada and he just left it here. So we're trying to sell it to get back the money for the work we did on it."

"How much do you want for it?" I asked.

"They're asking $800. All it needs is having that dent fixed up. The rest of it's in really good shape. It's not original, but it's all new work inside and the engine's been reconditioned all through."

"The thing is," I said, "I've got a TD already. But I know a bloke who's interested in buying one."

"I'd like to see somebody buy it," the attendant said. "It'll only go rusty if it's left here too long."

I was starting to get more and more drawn to the idea of having a matched pair of MG TDs, like a pair of Ming vases or duelling pistols, so I said goodbye quickly and went on down to the newsagents.

The day after that I drove past the service station again, and when I looked for the yellow bonnet in the line of cars I couldn't see it. T series MGs don't usually last too long on the market.

I was a bit surprised, though, at the way the attendant had picked me as a prospective buyer so quickly. He must have been able to see some sign of skilled appraisal or cool admiration in the way I was standing. In such ways do we MG fans reveal our true identities.

I bought my first MG TD in January, 1969, to celebrate leaving university. I saw the ad in the Herald classifieds, and I stopped off and looked it over on the way up to the mountains in my tired old sedan for the weekend. A week later I returned by train, paid for the car and drove off in it.

The TD couldn't be compared with the sedan. After driving it for a week or two, I was convinced that it couldn't be compared with anything. In those days of proud ownership and cautious handling I took my first steps along a path of no return.

The first TD was black with a red radiator grille. The trim inside was red, and the seats had black covers. It wasn't in original shape — it had a new dashboard with a number of instruments, such as a petrol gauge (which didn't work) and the big air filter was missing. The wood frame was cracked in a couple of places. The roof was old and fragile. But it scored highly in other departments.

It had been raced. I could see the outline of a circle on each door, where the number had been. The engine had been well tuned, and with a new set of rings it ran smoothly and very strongly. The steering was crisp and direct, which was a change from my old car — in that, you had to spin the wheel like the helm of a windjammer.

The roof didn't matter much. If I'd wanted to go on travelling in a closed box on wheels I wouldn't have bought a sports car. After a couple of months I

bought a tonneau, and folded the struts and canvas down for good. After a while I found that I could do without the windscreen too for most of the time, so I folded it down out of the way across the bonnet.

This meant that I had to learn to breathe in the slipstream. At first it wasn't too easy to suck in gulps of the chilly air hitting my face at 35 mph, or whatever. I can remember thundering along fine open stretches of road on winter mornings and ducking my face down behind the facia every half minute or so to snatch a breath. Driving was good training for skin-diving, or vice-versa. In the end I picked up the knack almost without realising it, as everyone must.

The TD's performance made everything else worthwhile. It wasn't something you could measure on the speedo, or over the standing quarter mile. TDs were obsolete when they were first built, and common family sedans were outclassing them by the end of the decade. It was a thing of style more than speed and quality more than quantity.

It was a combination of factors. It was looks — square front, close-set headlights between the forward-faired ends of the long mudguards, the businesslike jut of the lowered windscreen, the falling line of the tonneau behind, the sinister black finish. It was good handling and hard suspension. It was the vigorous and encouraging note of the engine.

And in the end, speed was part of it, too. She was powerful enough to take off at the lights in second, and on a good run on a clear road you could wind her up to 90 and beyond, right off the clock. Once, running into a head wind, she went over a long crest so fast that the air pressure building up under the windscreen started to lift it towards the vertical again. When the old lady lifted her skirts she could still run.

I kept her for four years, until January, 1973. By then she was starting to give more trouble than I could handle. The wood frame was decaying, and I couldn't afford the time or money to reconstruct her, so I put her up for sale.

Then I needed a new car. But four years of driving the TD had spoilt me, and I decided in the end that the only sort of car I could accept as a replacement was another classic MG. But how to find one?

Actually, one had already been found for me. Bill Lambourne, a CMF officer, had bought a TD and had it thoroughly refitted a few months after going for a run in mine. Now he had to sell it for domestic reasons. I knew that his TD was in good shape, and we made a swift bargain. I had a second TD.

This one was completely different from the first one. It was red, with a black radiator grille. The dashboard was original. The engine had been reconditioned and the frame had been restored. The body finish was good and the trim inside was plain but sound. Overall, I was very pleased with it. I still am.

The red TD does not perform as well as the black

one did. It's slower off the mark at the lights, and it doesn't run as easily or as fast going flat out. But it handles as well and so far — you always have to say so far — it has proved much more reliable.

If you hanker for the delights of classic sports car motoring, but are cursed with only a moderate income to meet the rising cost of living, then a T series MG is the only answer. Morgans are available but they're rather expensive, and everything else is in the province of the rich, idle hobbyist.

Australia was one of the main export markets for TCs, TDs and TFs, and now, after a quarter of a century, there are still an estimated 600 of them left in NSW alone. The would-be buyer keeps an eye on the classifieds every Saturday, ready to check out the two or three which will appear there. It IS still

possible to get a fairly sound, clean, registerable TD or TF for under $1000.

The MG T series began back in 1936, when the first 1292 cc push-rod-engined TAs rolled out of the Abingdon workshops. They soon proved themselves at more than 90 mph on the banked Brooklands track, and some were used as high-speed police patrol cars in the Home Counties.

TAs continued in production for three years, and then were superseded by the 1250 cc TB. But 1939 wasn't a good year to introduce a new model sports car. The war halted production within a few months, and no more MGs appeared until 1945.

In that year the MG TC opened the maker's post-war account, and became an immediate best-seller. It wasn't an astonishingly original design —

maintenance, a spring suspension system, a roomier body, and bumper bars fore and aft as a sop to progress. But the old square radiator, sweeping mudguards, cutaway doors and drop-flat windscreen were still fighting a rearguard action.

It was a losing fight, though. In 1954 the TF appeared, on a chassis similar to the TD's but with altered bodywork. The radiator shell was small and squashed-looking, the bonnet drooped to meet it and the headlights were faired into the flattish mudguards. For the T series, this half-hearted shot at streamlining was the end of the line.

A couple of years ago I listed all the T-series MGs I saw over a three-month period. TFs were the most common, then TCs and then TDs, with TFs making up nearly half of the total.

It is harder to say what the proportions are today, as all three varieties have become much rarer. I would reckon, though, that the number of TDs has fallen least, while TCs have become very rare sights indeed. It is anybody's guess why this should have happened. The missing cars can't all have been lost in smashes, or traded in and broken up. I think that a lot of them are laid up in garages being restored, and the ones which have been restored are too precious to drive very often.

This theory accounts for the change in proportion. For some reason, most MG fanciers rate the TD below both the TC and the TF. When you can pin them down over it, they mostly object to its disc wheels on aesthetic grounds. The TD also loses out historically, being neither the last of the real bone-shakers (which is the TC) nor the last of the T series (the TF). So TCs and TFs are more popular choices for restoration than TDs.

I am very happy with this state of affairs. I think the TD is in most ways the pick of the bunch. It isn't as starkly classical as the TC, but it is better mechanically (though slightly slower), and it is better looking than and mechanically equal to the TF. I will probably have to sell my TD soon, but at least I know that I won't have to shell out as much as I would for a TC or a TF when I buy my next one.

Have I thought of getting anything except another TD? Well, no, except maybe a TC at a good price. I could buy a car which was newer and shinier, which could go faster and give me softer seats to sit on and keep me dry. But those things don't count for much.

And what things do count? Well, partly it's financial. They're a lot of fun for $1000 or less, and they're good investments — from now on, the value of any T series car can only rise. And partly — or maybe mostly — it's because they give you more of what motoring really should be all about. And, not least, there's a sort of pride in driving one. Because you know that there are only a few hundred left, and no more where they came from.   *

closely based on the TB, with a new synchromesh gearbox and better finish — but it fitted very neatly into a large gap in the post-war market.

British enthusiasts were glad to see a new model MG out again after a six-year break, and they bought hundreds. Then a few were shipped to the US, and for some reason they started a fashion there. The Americans bought thousands.

We can thank the Americans for the survival of the T series until 1955. The MG company planned a streamlined replacement for the TC in 1949, but American dealers were shocked. An MG had to look like an MG, and the square radiator was the mark of the breed.

The TD, which appeared in January, 1950, was a compromise. It had solid disc wheels for ease of

'G's
HOME BREW

I do not own a flat tweed cap, neither do I have a predilection for gauntlets and voluminous overcoats of stormproofing properties. For that very reason I have always imagined myself to be excluded from the air-in-the-hair, scuttle-shaking world of post-vintage, pre-B sportycars. I thought that the above apparel, seasoned with Tattersall-check shirts, spotty cravats and horsey laughter over liberal potations of bitter, were as essential to the breed as cutaway doors and aeroscreens. Just goes to show how prejudiced and superficial my attitude can be at times, doesn't it? Still, I've revised my opinions after spending a very pleasant afternoon booming and looning round Cheddar and environs in a beaut of a 1950 MGTD complete with Shorrock blower and free fresh air. And the fact that neither the driver nor myself was wearing anything like the gear listed above detracted not one jot (or tittle, for that matter) from the performance of the car or the fun of the thrash.

Now that I know my Brutus brushed denims and platform shoes don't limit me to a life of saloon cars, there's only one thing that prevents me from becoming the proud owner of a character sports car, and that is — work. I simply dislike it, to the point of avoiding it whenever possible. My choice of personal transport is dictated by mechanical reliability and the availability of spares, which drops me right out of the TD stakes I'm afraid. Not to suggest that such a car is at all unreliable, but the age, coupled with a lack of the right bits and pieces, hints of dedication, inventiveness and, worst of all, work.

Mac Hawkins, owner of this month's feature car, certainly isn't scared of that terrible word, accepting the need to make up many of the parts for his TD as part and parcel of owning such a pleasing vehicle. And, my goodness, has he put in some graft? Makes me wince just to think of it.

Mac, a 29-year-old sales engineer from just outside Bridgwater, Zummerzet, is an MG fan of long standing, his love of the marque beginning at the age of 14 when he

would pilot his mother's PB up and down the driveway of his home. Mind you, this wasn't the only MG in the family as his grandfather owned a 1938 'SA — a sports saloon of some rarity. Unfortunately (and here comes that pun I promised you Mac) his granny made something of a boob by selling the car to a passing bra salesman for £30. (Sort of knocker down price? — Ed)

Good grief!

However, it wasn't until some years later that Mac became the possessor of his very own MG — the TD, in fact. He was serving in the army in Singapore when he made the acquaintance of a slinky piece of blonde. She just happened to have a TD she wanted to sell, and as Mac fancied the bird he bought the car — which seems to be an expensive way of doing things; I've always found a half dozen gin-and-tonics do the job just as well. Ah well, chacun a son goût as they say in French West Hartlepool.

So Mac ran the car around in Singapore for a few trouble-free months — trouble-free except, that is, for a mild ding at the front brought about by a passing monsoon. When Mac was demobbed he shipped the car back to GB, hence the C-registration, and decided to tidy it up a little, starting with the bent front bumper. Well, off it came, and a few more faults were discovered — a process which continued until the car had been stripped down almost to the bare chassis. Like the Morgan series of cars, the body panels on the early MGs were hung on wooden battens, which in this case were in a sorry state, requiring immediate replacement. Rather than hunt around for unroadworthy TDs with woodwork in good nick, Mac opted to make the necessary pieces himself and renail the panels. Yes indeed, nails. That's how the body sticks on to the framework. The panels fold over the battens and are nailed on from the inside, which means that to restore an MGTD one has to be as much of a carpenter as an engineer, and stand the risk of splinters and flattened thumbs. Makes a change I suppose. The hardest part of this job was reshaping the panels to the framework without causing dimpling or distortion.

While the chassis was exposed it was daubed with underbody protection and hydraulic jacks from an MG Y-type were fitted. In case you don't know the Y-type had jacks attached to the four corners of the chass, operated by a hydraulic pump system under the bonnet. This meant that to change a wheel or suchlike all you had to do was attach the pump lever to the unit and heave away — whereupon, like magic, the little motor car performed a neat levitation act. A hand control enabled front, rear or both to be lifted, and a reverse twist of the valve knob dropped the lot back to the ground again. A fabulous rig and one which Mac fitted to the TD with no trouble at all. Shame that similar systems aren't still employed; they would save a lot of grovelling around with hand jacks and those nasty ratchet handles which never seem to ratch properly.

All the body panels were rubbed down to bare metal, restored where necessary, and the original BRG paintwork replaced with Tartan Red. Straightening the front wings was rather a work-up, taking Mac ages before they were perfectly matched and accurate. All the bright metal parts, such as radiator shell, bumpers, luggage rack, etc., were rechromed, and new hood, side-screens and tonneau were made up.

Bucket seats made up from a couple of Dennis lorry items were placed in the cockpit, although Mac has retained the originals for originality's sake. The interior is basically red and black, with new carpets, clip-on beading at the top of all panels, and a revised dash. This latter item has been revamped in order to feed a little more information to the driver. An accurate petrol gauge has been fitted, plus new speedo, tacho, oil pressure/water temp gauge, oil temp gauge, ammeter, pressure/vacuum gauge, battery condition indicator, rheostat switches for heater and panel lights, Butler map light and petrol and oil warning lights. Direction indicators have been installed, in conjuction with horn, dip and main beam and spot light switches. The original steering wheel has been retained, and a two-way switch operates a choice of air-horns or Klaxon.

Now, scuffling back under the car again we discover that not only has the chassis been undersealed, it's also got a few new bits dangling from't. Brand spanking springs and shockers are fitted (although the front nearside shock has recently become a bit knackered). New brakes, hoses and cables make sure it stops, while equally recent bearings help the wheels round. The only additions to improve roadholding (which is already surprisingly good for a car of this era) is an anti-roll bar at the front and 165 x 15 Goodyear G800's all round.

The transmission is most interesting: the rear axle has been completely overhauled and rebuilt, but the demon bit is the addition of a Laycock overdrive unit. This came from an old Standard Vanguard gearbox and is mated to the original MG box by means of the Vanguard main shaft which was first shortened and resplined. A normal $3\frac{1}{2}$in propshaft coupling is used and the shaft itself is a shortened and modified Land Rover unit meeting the o/d via a Hardy Spicer joint. The speedo cable now comes from the tail of the o/d casing and is therefore a bit longer than standard. Mounting is by means of Morris 1000 torsion bars welded to the overdrive and bolted to either side of the main chassis rails, and through rubber engine mounting blocks onto a 2in x 1in steel crossmember bolted to the chassis. Overdrive is now available on all four forward gears, making the car much more driveable — not to mention economical.

The construction of this transmission really was a sod, though, and Mac still has the scars to prove it. Scars which were inflicted when he caught his sweater sleeve in a rapidly twirling Hardy Spicer. Mind you, the end result is certainly highly commendable and worth all the bother involved. Full marks, Mac.

Now to the engine. This was, naturally, completely rebuilt, and bored out plus 20 thou. The crankshaft, conrods, pistons, flywheel and clutch have all been balanced by Brabham Racing. The cylinder head is from an MG TF, giving a compression ratio of about 8.6:1 — this has to be low because of the blower. Blower? Oh yes, there's a large, long-nosed Shorrock sitting next to the engine, drawing fuel through a $1\frac{1}{2}$in SU carb and dumping it in the combustion chambers at a boost pressure of 6 psi. The pre-blower head was a planed and polished TD job giving a c/r of 9.3:1.

By pleasant coincidence the supercharger was found laying around in a friend's attic. Said friend didn't know what kind of car it was for, but craft Mac did and bought it for a knock-down price. A few quid spent at Allards on an overhaul, and there it was, good as new and raring to blow. However, the standard exhaust manifold left much to be desired to it was chopped for a Derrington extractor job.

To cope with the extra oomph provided by a half-race camshaft the head was fitted with 150lb valve springs, rebuilt rocker gear and larger valves. To prettify it somewhat the rocker cover and valve guide covers were chromed.

On the electrical side of things there's a new sports coil, a symmetrical cam distributor and a heavy duty battery. The wiring has been renewed throughout and new sealed beam headlights incorporated up front.

Cooling is carried out by a new rad (with new hoses, of course) fitted with a rad blind which is operated by a pull-ring in the cockpit quite efficiently.

All in all a most pleasing little beast and one which does credit to its owner. Mac reckons that the power output is around 95 bhp, and claims a 0 to 60 time of 10.5 secs and a top speed in excess of 100 mph. Not bad for a car which first saw light of day in 1950. ∎

MG.TD on the road

While perhaps lacking the simplicity of line possessed by its forebears, the MG TD nevertheless acquitted itself well as a nimble two-seater car of character. Paul Skilleter looks at the TD through 1974 eyes.

IT would be a truism to say that the two letters "MG" are a near-perfect definition of the term "sports car", a state of affairs which was undoubtedly established—in America at least—during the early forties. Even now, ask someone to elucidate on the image conjured up by these letters and the chances are that you will be given a description of a small red car with square lines, separate wings, and a stubby tail with a spare wheel stuck on it. The MG TD conforms completely with this specification, anachronistic as it might have been for a 1949 car, although a look under its skin reveals that a process of civilisation had set in—for the TD was the first, production Midget to feature that 'modern' invention, independent front suspension. In fact it could be said that the TD

differed more from its immediate predecessor than had any of the Midget MGs up to that date, going right back to the M-type of 1928.

The TD MG took over from the TC, introduced just after the war and which was little more than a continuation of the pre-war TB, which itself had a lineage dating back to the Series M Midget. It is to the TC that much of the British motor industry owes a great deal, for it introduced the American motorist to the delights of the true sports car, a type of vehicle of which he had hitherto been ignorant. Naturally it educated him even more to the particular merits of the MG sports car and so far as Abingdon was concerned, it was merely a question of making enough.

The fact that the Midget was even more old fashioned in the United States than in Great Britain, and was thus an even stronger contrast to the every day four-seater saloon in common use, was probably an advantage rather than a disadvantage, as the difference only served to emphasise the little car's character and looks. Its ability to leave behind home-produced cars of up to three times the horse-power at the slightest suggestion of a corner was a novelty that was not tired of—even though one really needed an XK 120 to enjoy a similar superiority in a straight line. But apart from this almost undreamed of manoeuvreability, it was probably the looks of the car which got most Americans.

The MG TD was intended to continue a modest but highly successful sales pattern abroad but with a few more creature comforts thrown into the mixture, of the sort which it was thought the American buyer wanted. At the same time, expediency demanded that protracted design and development was out, so as F. Wilson McComb relates in his "Story of the MG Sports Car", the TD was "designed" by simply taking a Y-type saloon chassis (the $1\frac{1}{4}$-litre 'Y' saloon with its independent front suspension had been introduced in 1947), reducing its wheelbase to that of the TC, and mounting a TC body on it. Hey presto, a sports car with fully sorted independent front suspension in one go.

To be fair, when the MG TD was released for public consumption in January 1950 it differed a little from the prototype described. The chassis was still basically that of the 'Y' saloon, shortened by 5

Bill Clark's 1953 example; disc wheels dilute the original Midget concept slightly — the later TF had different hubs allowing wire wheels to be fitted.

inches and swept over the rear axle instead of underneath it; the chassis frame itself had boxed side members braced by tubular cross members. Unique to the TD though was a steel hoop which followed the contours of the scuttle, adding stiffness to the structure and, according to *The Autocar*, providing "protection for the occupants if the car should be overturned during some hectic trial"—a sort of shoulder-level roll over bar. The independent front suspension employed upper and lower wishbones, connected at their apex by stub-axle and swivel-pin. The top wishbone had its inward mountings in the main bearings of a double-piston hydraulic damper. Springing itself was by a coil under compression between the two wishbones, all à la Y-type saloon. The TD's steering was from the same car, a precise rack and pinion system which had the advantage of being easily transposed to provide either right or left hand drive—but with the grave disadvantage of ruling out the possibility of fitting wire wheels, as the projection of the steering arms made it necessary to adopt concave steel disc wheels. At the rear of the car, half-elliptic leaf springs were used, in conjunction with hydraulic lever-type shock absorbers.

Brakes were Lockheed hydraulic, the new two leading shoe (front) system being an improvement of the TC's equipment; handbrake was of the fly-off pattern. Powering the TD was the 1250cc, 66.5×90mm, four cylinder engine as of yore, developing 54 bhp at 5,200 rpm on a 7.25:1 CR; it breathed through two semi-downdraught SU carburettors. The wide-ratio four-speed gearbox was another in-

heritance from the 'Y' saloon, while the final drive ratio of 5.125:1 was similar to that of the TC—although the later car's smaller wheels (15 inch as opposed to 19 inch) lowered the top-gear road speed from 15.5 mph to 14.5 mph.

Somehow the look of the new car was different, even though the theme remained exactly the same—it appeared lower, wider and less angular than before, although actually the hood-up height remained unchanged and it was only four inches wider across the body. A greater area of mudguarding and bumpers fore and aft also served to add an air of civilisation, unwanted in many cases—what, an MG with bumpers and no wire wheels? The purists reeled. But they were in the minority, as the TD was an immediate success in the States and its sales soon overtook those of the TC. Theoretically the car was available in this country too, but those remaining on native soil were numbered in hundreds as opposed to the thousands shipped overseas (TD production eventually totalled some 29,600). Its home market price on announcement in late 1949 was £445, or £596 with purchase tax, although this had crept up to over £800 before the TD was superseded by the slightly controversial TF series towards the end of 1953.

The MG Midget has always been nippy rather than fast, and with an extra 1½ cwt to lug about the TD was no faster than its similarly powered predecessor—though surprisingly it wasn't much slower either. *The Motor* recorded a top speed of 77.2 mph mean, with 60 mph coming up in 21.3 seconds (the TC reached that speed

in 21.1 seconds). The new chassis was praised in contemporary road tests, the TC's harsh ride being banished—"Gone entirely is the old sports car harshness, the ride now giving a combination of firmness and freedom from road shocks . . ." quoth *The Motor* in February 1950. Handling hadn't deteriorated as the same magazine thought there was a "definite advance in general roadholding and cornering" particularly on bumpy surfaces. Summing up its report, *The Motor* said: ". . . the TD proved to be a car which, like its forerunners, one took to with enthusiasm and parted with reluctance, the only difference being that both the enthusiasm and the reluctance were greater than before."

It was certainly with enthusiasm that I approached a drive of Mr Bill Clark's MG TD; the only reluctance being engendered through my learning that the car to be sampled was probably *the* premier 'concours' TD in the country. But I need not have worried; immaculate OKD 121 certainly is, but it is no fingers-off glass-case museum special and has actually been driven some 17,000 miles in all weathers since its painstaking body-off-chassis rebuild by Bill Clark in 1970. Which is as it should be of course.

It would have been difficult to have chosen a better car with which to review the MG TD in the perspective of 1974; every effort has been made to keep the car totally original, and all moving parts have been carefully refurbished—the car simply drove like new, with no evidence of slackness or wear anywhere. In fact the whole car felt considerably less old fashioned than either it looked or I had imagined. Acceleration was smooth if not particularly quick, with the engine surprisingly willing to slog at low rpm in any gear or to wind happily up towards where the red line ought to be on the tachometer, but isn't on the TD (it is safe to the last figure on the dial, 6,000rpm, although I didn't use that much). It was, however, in the region of ride and handling where the pleasant surprises lay; the car's behaviour over less than perfect surfaces was easily up to the standards set by most small saloons of today, understandable I suppose in view of the similarity in weight. To be quite honest I didn't try 'earholing' the TD despite a plentiful supply of the right ingredients (bright sunshine, hood down, and deserted Oxfordshire lanes) as I do possess some respect for other people's feelings; but under Bill Clark's encouragement I wound the little car up to an indicated 78mph or so, and entered a couple of corners quickly enough to take as read the moderate oversteering characteristics talked about in contemporary road tests—and which probably accounts for the responsive, nimble feeling of the car around the twisting low speed roads for which it is ideal.

Actually OKD 121 has a contemporary 'Stage 2' tuning kit which gives it a slightly brisker performance and a genuine 80 mph-plus top speed, thanks to a higher compression ratio and larger (TF) valves. In summation, I would say that the TD equated well with the performance, ride and handling of the 1256cc Vauxhall Viva in which I was forced to journey up to Oxford (there being a distinct and much felt dearth of running 'classic' machinery in the modest Skilleter stable at this time). This surely, does not reflect all that badly on a moderately priced, mass-produced two-seater of 25 years ago. ●

Above: OKD 121 being stripped for its rebuild. Over £1,400 was spent on parts alone.
Below: Engine bay, showing the two 1¼" SUs. Petrol consumption is about 23 mpg.

Closeness of wheel to seats is certainly one dating feature; screen folds flat for competitions, and the TD introduced many to racing.

BROOKLANDS BOOKS

MGA & MGB

MG MGB 1962-1970

A total of 10 road tests, plus comparison tests, a 45,000 mile report and used car tests together with articles on new model introductions, tuning, Le Mans, the Taurus and Janspeed MGB, and manufacturing. All model MGB roadsters up to 1970 are covered including the 3 & 5 bearing engines and the automatic.
100 Large Pages.

MG MGB 1970-1980

Over thirty articles covering the following topics. Road tests, comparison tests, used car tests, new model introductions, design proposals, history, choosing a used MGB, rebuilding, supertuning, race preparation, service testing, investment and driving impressions, models covered include the MK I & MK II & MK III. Roadsters with manual & automatic drive.
100 Large Pages.

MG CARS 1959-1962

This book deals with all MG models in production between 1959 and 1962, and there are comprehensive road tests on the MGB from Autocar and Car & Driver and introductory articles from Autosport and Motor. Other models covered in this book include the MGA, Midget, Magnette 1100 & articles cover road tests, road research reports, racing, used car tests and history.
100 Large Pages.

MG MGB GT 1965-1980

A total of 8 road tests and 31 articles covering the GT version of this popular classic car. Topics covered are, buying secondhand, used car tests, comparison tests, driving impressions, 12,000 and 24,000 mile reports, new model introductions, factory visits and drivers reports. All MGB GT models are reported on including the Berlinette, the Castello and the V8.
100 Large Pages.

MG MGA 1955-1962

The most comprehensive Brooklands title on the MGA. Some 8 road tests are included in the 35 articles. Other stories cover driving reports, new model introductions, a used car test, record breaking, Le Mans, a 30,000m report and a comparison test between the TR3A and Twin-Cam. Models covered are the roadster, coupé, EX 179, 181 and 182, plus the 1600, MkII, and Twin-Cam.
100 Large Pages.

MGA Collection No. 1 (1955-1982)

A total of 24 articles drawn from the US, Britain and Australia. Besides 6 road tests there are articles on touring, history, record breaking and new model reports, plus advice on buying a used model, rebuilding and tuning. Models covered are the roadster, coupé, 1600, MkII, Twin-Cam and EX 181.
70 Large Pages.

These soft-bound volumes in the 'Brooklands Books' series consist of reprints of original road test reports and other articles that appeared in leading motoring journals during the periods concerned. Fully illustrated with photographs and cut-away drawings, the articles contain road impressions, performance figures, specifications, etc. None of the articles appears in more than one book. Sources include Autocar, Autosport, Car, Car & Driver, Cars & Car Conversions, Motor, Motor Racing, Modern Motor, Road Test, Road & Track and Wheels. Fascinating to read, the books are also invaluable as sources of historical reference and as practical aids to enthusiasts who wish to restore their cars to original condition.

From specialist booksellers or, in case of difficulty, direct from the distributors:
BROOKLANDS BOOK DISTRIBUTION, 'HOLMERISE', SEVEN HILLS ROAD,
COBHAM, SURREY KT11 1ES, ENGLAND. Telephone: Cobham (09326) 5051
MOTORBOOKS INTERNATIONAL, OSCEOLA, WISCONSIN 54020, USA.
Telephone: 715 294 3345 & 800 826 6600

MG TC 1945-1949

Some 35 stories from Britain the US and Australia are brought together to form a profile of the first post-war MG Midget, the TC. Included are road tests, used car tests, driving impressions, plus articles on touring, record breaking, racing, restoration, rebuilding, and repair in general. A 1000 mile test is undertaken which ends at the factory at Abingdon. More recent articles written during the 70s and 80s cover the TCs current position and comment on how it fits into the classic car scene.
100 Large Pages.

MG TD 1949-1953

The development of the MG TD is trace through 34 articles drawn from the leading journals of Australia, the US and Britain. Included are road tests on the Series I and II, a comparison test v. the TC, 2000 and 35,000 mile reports, together with stories on tuning, touring, rebuilding, racing, and record breaking. A used car test is also reprinted plus a fascinating report on a journey from Bombay to London.
100 Large Pages.

MG TF 1953-1955

Reports from Britain, the US, Ireland and Australia lead us through the production life of the TF Midget. Articles cover road tests of the 1250, 1500 and supercharged cars, comparison tests against the TC and TD models, new model announcements, plus stories on tuning, racing, restoration, history and a visit to Abingdon. Also included is an 8 page data sheet outlining all servicing requirements of the TF.
100 Large Pages.

These soft-bound volumes in the 'Brooklands Books' series consist of reprints of original road test reports and other articles that appeared in leading motoring journals during the periods concerned. Fully illustrated with photographs and cut-away drawings, the articles contain road impressions, performance figures, specifications, etc. None of the articles appears in more than one book. Sources include Autocar, Autosport, Car, Car & Driver, Cars & Car Conversions, Motor, Motor Racing, Modern Motor, Road Test, Road & Track and Wheels. Fascinating to read, the books are also invaluable as sources of historical reference and as practical aids to enthusiasts who wish to restore their cars to original condition.

From specialist booksellers or, in case of difficulty, direct from the distributors:
BROOKLANDS BOOK DISTRIBUTION, 'HOLMERISE', SEVEN HILLS ROAD,
COBHAM, SURREY KT11 1ES, ENGLAND. Telephone: Cobham (09326) 5051
MOTORBOOKS INTERNATIONAL, OSCEOLA, WISCONSIN 54020, USA.
Telephone: 715 294 3345 & 800 826 6600